Is There Not a Cause?

We Are Here—Because We Are Not There!

JAY R. LEACH

Order this book online at www.trafford.com
or email orders@trafford.com

Most Trafford titles are also available at major online book retailers.

New King James Version (NKJV)

Scripture taken from the New King James Version®. Copyright © 1982
by Thomas Nelson. Used by permission. All rights reserved.

Print information available on the last page.

ISBN: 978-1-4907-8459-5 (sc)
ISBN: 978-1-4907-8461-8 (hc)
ISBN: 978-1-4907-8460-1 (e)

Library of Congress Control Number: 2017913964

Trafford rev. 09/29/2017

www.trafford.com
North America & international
toll-free: 1 888 232 4444 (USA & Canada)
fax: 812 355 4082

BOOKS BY JAY R. LEACH

How Should We Then Live
Behold the Man
The Blood Runs Through It
Drawn Away
Give Me Jesus
A Lamp unto My Feet
Grace that Saves
The Narrow Way
Radical Restoration in the Church
Manifestation of the True Children of God
According to Pattern
Battle Cry
Is there not a Cause?

DEDICATION

To our children
Jenel [David], Sonja [Andrew], Tonia [Darryl],
Jay [Tonya], Jayson [Luetica]

"Give ear O my people, to my law
Incline your ear to the words of my mouth,
So that the generation to come would know them,
The children who would be born,
That they may arise and declare them to their children."

– Psalm 78:1, 6

PSALM I

A PSALM OF THE TWO WAYS

Blessed is the man that walketh not in
counsel of the ungodly, nor
standeth in the way of sinners,
nor sitteth in the seat of the scornful.

But his delight is in the law of the LORD;
and in his law doth he meditate day and night.

And he shall be like a tree planted by the rivers
of water, that bringeth forth
his fruit in his season; his leaf also shall
not wither; and whatsoever he doeth
shall prosper.

The ungodly are not so: but are like
the chaff which the wind driveth away.

Therefore the ungodly shall not
stand in the judgment,
nor sinners in the congregation of the righteous.

For the LORD knoweth the way of
the righteous:
but the way of the ungodly shall perish.

– Psalm I (KJV)

CONTENTS

SECTION I

THE POWER OF PURPOSE

SECTION II

WE ARE HERE

SECTION III

BECAUSE WE ARE NOT THERE

SECTION IV

WHERE DO WE GO FROM HERE?

SECTION V

GETTING IT RIGHT

INTRODUCTION

This work began with an earthly crisis and ends with hope of eternal glory. My motive for writing this book is two-fold: First to help people struggling with the subtly upheavals and massive changes experienced in the culture and the local churches of this country over the past sixty or so years. Satan knows that he cannot defeat or destroy the church of the Living God; but he has been working furiously to distract as many people from God's strategic redemptive plan as he possibly can. Many of the local churches have caved in to his bluffs and they are silently retreating inside the four walls of the church building at the insistence of two of his most formidable weapons spiritual illiteracy and biblical illiteracy.

Increasingly these churches are assimilating so much of the secular agenda that many of the members can be classified: *practical* secularists, atheists, consumerists, and acute narcissists; as a result of the churches' subtle turn from the authority of the Holy Scriptures to the authority of the culture. At the same time a progressive omission of the Holy Spirit, His ministries and a growing rejection of a biblical worldview for a progressively secular view. The secular view is carefully produced and engineered by the now-openly secular media, self-experience, science, reason, and carefully crafted secular-based public educational systems, in which the theory of evolution is placed above creation truth. This deception is now ingrained beginning in nursery school through graduate school at every level. Rather than standing firm in the righteousness of God in Christ, and the revealed truths of God-centered Christianity. Since the 16th century [Reformation] a great percentage of the people sitting in the pews of local churches have favored a progressive pseudo-religious Christianity which requires neither the supernatural nor meaningful commitment to Christ and His Church.

True Christian service and living righteous lives must begin with right thinking.[1] The church is God's idea; and just as it was with His instructions to Moses for the construction, dedication, and service of the tabernacle, all were according to God's plan, pattern, and instructions.[2] He left absolutely nothing to man's distorted imagination, because of his sin-generated depravity; nor did God ask him what he thought about His plan. His instructions demanded humility, faithfulness and obedience according to pattern ["lest you die!"].

Jesus Christ founded the Church, according to pattern, "Upon this Rock I will build My Church" (Matthew 16:18). He purchased it with His own blood (Acts 20:28), and intimately identifies Himself with it (Acts 9:4). The church is the body of Christ (1 Corinthians 12:12, 27; Ephesians 1:22-23; 4:12; 520-30; Colossians 1:18, 24; 3:15), the dwelling place of His Holy Spirit and the chief instrument for glorifying God in the world (Ezekiel 36:22-38; Ephesians 3:10). He provided the Holy Spirit and Scripture guided plan and strategy for the church; which *requires* that each participating person have a new birth from above, and a personal intimate relationship with the Lord, Jesus Christ, our Savior.

In the tabernacle the "legal sacrifice" was killed and prepared by the priests according to pattern and placed on the brazen altar to be consumed by fire which originated in heaven. The "living sacrifice" of the New Covenant is in glorious contrast to the dead "legal sacrifice" of the Old Covenant. The death of the "Lamb of God which takes away the sins of the world" settled that (John 1:29). Today under grace [God's unmerited favor], Christians are instructed in Romans 12:1-5 to:

- Present your body *a living sacrifice, holy,* **and acceptable unto God** *which is your reasonable service.* Emphasis added throughout.
- Be not conformed to this world [don't let the world mold you according to their ungodly values and worldview] which is designed to do away with God, Christ, the things of God and Christians [replacing creation and transformation].

- Be transformed by the renewing of your mind through the Holy Spirit and the knowledge of the truth [God's Word].
- Don't think of yourself more highly than you ought to think.

Christians who fail in life are those who have first failed at the altar. How? By refusing to *fully* surrender themselves to the leadership of Christ.

The motive for *full* surrender and dedication is love; the apostle Paul did not say, "I command you" but "I beseech [urge] you, because of what God has already done for you." We do not serve the Lord in order to receive mercies, because we already have them. No, we serve Him because we love and appreciate Him. That is basic!

Authentic full surrender and dedication is the presenting of our body and our soul [comprised of our mind, will, and affections] to God day after day. It is a daily *yielding* of your body to Him, having the *mind renewed* by the Spirit and the Word of God, and *surrendering* the will ["not my will Father, but your will"], through faithfulness, reverence, prayer and obedience [individually and corporately].

Every Christian can be classified as either a conformer[3] living for and like the world, or a transformer,[4] daily becoming more Christlike throughout their lives as part of a Bible-believing Christian Church. In II Corinthians 3:18 we are told that we are transformed as we allow the Spirit to reveal Christ to us through the Word of God. Jesus Christ by His Holy Spirit dwells in every true believer; the church is the aggregate body to which Jesus has given His life.

If you touch Christians, you have touched Christ. Christians are a sacramental people. A sacrament is a means of grace; it is a mysterious symbol which bears the presence of Christ through which believers encounter Christ. In view of Ephesians 1:23, in some mysterious sense the church as the body of Christ fills or completes Christ. In other words, Jesus is the Head of the church – but a head without a body is no good. Let's turn that around, the church is the container, and Jesus is the one who fills it with life.

My *second* motivation for writing is having celebrated my seventy-seventh birthday; I realize that many of the local churches in America are in real trouble with little or no cultural relevance, having shifted from God's plan and strategy of Bible-centered authority and worship to that of an entertainment-centeredness, or an emotion-centeredness, or a social action-centeredness, or a prosperity-centeredness [investment giving]. I hear many young and older preachers these days saying that God is going to do a "new thing," "Why should He?" Among His last Words of instruction to us was "This is My beloved Son in whom I am well pleased ...... Hear Him!"

Recent Barna research has reported that pastors are remaining longer; that same research disclosed that there are more pastors 65 years of age and beyond in this country than pastors 40 years old and younger. Why is that? I believe it's due the churches' move from Bible-centeredness for a foundation to one or more of those we covered above.

I pray that senior ministers will take advantage of this opportunity and reconsider their recliner and retirement-travel options; and chose to mentor, help, inform, train and equip the next generation of preachers and other Christian workers with "the faith" once delivered to the saints – bringing them into the knowledge of the truth and a renewed practical appreciation for the power of the gospel of Christ. Expository preaching for example is almost as extinct as the fire and brimstone preaching of so-called yesteryear.

It is apparent from recent research concerning the millennia generation, that many young people between the ages of 18 and 34, have left the church and have little or no interest in Christianity. Yet, other statistics show that many of them are eagerly sharing their faith – they love to physically praise the Lord; and many are seeking a deeper spiritual walk with God. I favor the second report, don't you? When we offer to be mentors or spiritual fathers and spiritual mothers to young people, many of them are eager to get on board. Christ's kingdom mission for the church is still valid:

"Go therefore and make disciples of all nations, baptizing them in the name of the Father and the Son and the Holy Spirit, teaching them to observe all that I have commanded you; and lo, I am with you always, unto to the end of the age" (Matthew 28:19-20).

Every Christian individually and corporately must reconnect with the strategic redemptive plan given by God Himself. God's *ultimate* goal for every Christian is *Christlikeness,* the first work for those attempting to carry out the Great Commission.

Neither you nor I can just wish for Christlikeness, conger it up, or buy it. It has to be developed in each of us over time through our new nature by the Holy Spirit. Spiritual gifts are given to the believer by the Holy Spirit, but the fruit of the Spirit is developed and grown; which requires time, faithfulness, loving care and protection. If we read the *red* in the Bible we will see and hear Jesus speak in His own words through the Holy Spirit.

The Holy Spirit working through Paul listed those Christlike character qualities [fruit of the Spirit] in Galatians 5:22, 23 that make all true believers one in Christ – as we fully yield ourselves to the Word of God and the Holy Spirit yielding to Him as He develops this spiritual fruit within us.

Christian character is not mere moral, legal or political correctness no matter how together we might think we are, but we must possess and manifest the Christlike character through the Spirit of God within us. Don't let the life of Christ end with you.

Later in chapter 19, I will deal heavily with the fact that the leadership must give the church back to the people. Every member has the responsibility of being one of Christ's agents of reconciliation moving the church from adding believers to the kingdom to being multipliers of believers through teaching others who in turn will do the same (study carefully 2 Timothy 2:2).

God desires that each Christian mature in Christlikeness, and reproduces His or her life in others. The fruit comprise nine graces; without which we can not be effective disciples. Actually attempting to be a disciple in our own strength can cause irreparable damage and confusion simply because the flesh will keep popping up and contradict profession, by revealing our true character; therefore, let's look to the Lord for these authentic biblical fruit graces:

The first three graces display the character of the believer's inward state, which are not determined by circumstances, but in spite of circumstances:

- Love
- Joy
- Peace

The second three graces display the believer's character expression toward others [people]:

- Longsuffering
- Gentleness
- Kindness

The third three graces display the believer's character in expression toward God:

- Faith
- Meekness
- Temperance

Placed together they present a moral portrait of Christ, and may be taken as the apostle's explanation in Galatians 2:20 *"Not I, but Christ,"* and additionally as a definition of *"fruit"* in John 15:1-4:

"I am the true vine, and My Father is the vinedresser. Every branch in Me that does not bear fruit He takes away; and every branch that bears fruit He prunes, that it may bear more fruit ...... Abide in Me, and I in you. As the branch cannot bear fruit of itself, unless it abides in the vine, neither can you unless you abide in Me."

Jesus says, "Abide in Me." Abide means "to remain" or "dwell in." The evidence of salvation is continuance in service to the Lord and His teaching. Then Jesus said to those Jews that believed in Him,

"If you abide in My word, you are My disciples indeed. And you shall know the truth and the truth shall make you free" (see John 8:31-32).

Pastors must lead *all* of the church in recommitting themselves to following Christ through obedience to the Spirit and the Scriptures as true mature disciples serving in their giftedness to the glory of God:

1. The first step in the progress is belief in Jesus Christ as the Messiah and Son of God.
2. Perseverance in obedience to the Holy Spirit and Scripture (see Galatians 5:22, 23; Matthew 28:19-20), and the Great Commission.
3. A genuinely saved and obedient disciple of the Lord Jesus Christ will seek and know divine truth and freedom from sin (v. 34).

Genuine disciples individually and corporately who faithfully hold fast, obey and practice Jesus' teachings have both the Father and the Son. Pastors and other church leaders must heed what Jesus said and establish themselves and their local churches on the Enduring Truth, Jesus Christ. Ray Steadman wrote so beautifully [5] in his book, *Body Life:* "The life of Jesus continues to be manifested among people; but no longer through an individual physical body, limited to one place on earth, but through a complex, corporate body called the church."

Jay R. Leach
Fayetteville, NC

SECTION I

THE POWER OF PURPOSE

CHAPTER ONE

THE CHURCH ON PURPOSE

"But seek first the kingdom of God, and His righteousness, and all these things shall be added unto you" (Matthew 6:33).

The principles and purpose of the church has remained the same since Christ founded it 2000 years ago, but the methodology for achieving that purpose has changed throughout the generations. A church is effective so long as it single-mindedly pursues the purpose God has ordained for it. That is, proclaiming the gospel audibly, and living Christ-like lives together in local congregations making the gospel visible (see John 13:34-35). However, methodology [the how-to] must change and adept to the relevancy of the times and environment without compromise.

THE CHURCH IS THE GOSPEL MADE VISIBLE!

While a very noticeable cloud of despair has settled over the non-Christian world, due to the failure of mankind's idol-gods, a vacuum is left ready for the gospel of Christ to fill. It is a time of great opportunity for the Church of the Living God; whenever and wherever foundations are shaken doors open unexpectedly. Depending on who is talking; today is perhaps the greatest opportunity since its founding, for the church to shine not inside the four walls – but outside in the streets and marketplace where it was birthed.

The authority of Christ compels Christians individually and corporately to study the Bible's teaching on the church. So many congregations act as if the Bible comprises only the four gospels and the Book of Revelation and therefore they reject the Old Testament, the Book of Acts and the General and Pauline Epistles as irrelevant Church History.

ITS TIME TO WAKE UP

The church in America has been compared to a rich sleeping giant with great and powerful potential. This conclusion has been reached in view of church history. However, the church around the world has proven to be resilient and tough throughout the centuries. Notice the stand made by the Coptic Christians in Egypt, and other parts of the Middle East. God is still the Pilot! Due to the present crisis of decline many Christian communities have produced through prayerful innovation, some new models, while remaining spiritual and doctrinally pure.

Remember, the church is to make Jesus *visible* to the world, and particularly individual Christians in their areas of influence to include family, community and the marketplace. How? The same way Jesus made God the Father *visible* by being full of grace and truth. Therefore the Church is *called* and *empowered* to make the ascended Christ *visible* in the world today by being absolutely full of grace and truth. The apostle Paul says,

"God raised us up with Christ and seated us with Him in the heavenly realms in Christ Jesus, in order that in the coming ages now and forever He might show the incomparable riches of His grace, expressed in His kindness to us in Christ Jesus. For it is by grace you have been saved, through faith – and this not from yourselves, it is the gift of God – not by works, so that no one can boast" (Ephesians 2:6-9).

4

That is, God has poured out His grace on us in order that we might, in turn, be **demonstrators** of His grace to others. In other words, when people see God's grace in us, **they will see Jesus in us [Christlikeness]**, just like people saw God in the fullness of Jesus' grace. As the body of Christ, the universal recipients of God's grace, we visibly represent *the work and person of Jesus* to the world. The glory of God is seen both in the person of the Son and in the *collective witness of the church!* This is the authentic Christian Church, the body of Christ. I say again, Christlikeness is the ultimate goal of God's redemptive plan for every born again Christian – and nothing less. Emphasis added.

The expectations of Christ for the local churches and individuals who have bowed to the new pseudo-progressive religious Christianity by compromise are impossible to complete. Such churches on many moral issues have assimilated the culture's secular worldview. People are getting sick and tired of deceptive sugar substitutes. They are looking for the real thing!

Church leadership must be ever mindful that *wrong* ecclesiastical teaching and practices result in:

- the loss of the fear of God
- the Bible is no longer center
- they no longer discern the will of God
- unless revival comes – soon they lose the gospel
- they are standing on the wrong foundation

As the tides are changing more and more people are seeking an authentic Biblical and Christ-centered spiritual life. As the numbers grow daily, millions of people are *not* finding the kind of spiritual vitality in the local churches today that Jesus described. People want the simple, powerful, transformation evidently found in the New Testament.

The higher echelons of the various denominations' causes are loosing support at the local grassroots levels because too many of their causes are just plain materially and secularly oriented. The local churches and more specifically individual Christians are the focal point of the kingdom of God – what happens at their level is ultimately important. Certainly God's will, should spearhead all thoughts and actions concerning any process of change, but we must keep in mind the fact that God has made human beings active agents in these spiritual matters.

As for conditions of change under human control – the outcomes vary. The influence of God or Satan on the matter is dependent upon the variableness of human spirituality and interaction. Without revival of the Christ-centered authority and worship all efforts are our own and fruitless. Today many local churches are drifting into currents of pragmatism, assuming that the immediate response of non-Christians is the key indicator of success. Blindly they can't see that:

- Christianity is being very rapidly disowned in the culture at large.
- Evangelism is characterized as intolerant.
- Portions of biblical doctrine are classified as "hate speech."
- More and more congregations are conforming to the culture, which if not countered could mean the loss of the gospel *again!*
- As long as numbers and buildings remain the primary indicators of church health, the truth will be compromised.
- For authenticity churches must once again begin measuring success not in terms of numbers, but in terms of fidelity to the Scriptures.
- Those churches that truthfully persevered throughout the generations promote themselves as "relevant."

EVALUATION OF PURPOSE

In proper evaluation of the local church's purpose, some aspects of the congregational life and work are negotiable and open to change and some are non negotiable because of biblical mandate. Therefore, any change must be preceded by pursuing the answers to two very important questions; which must be asked of the congregation [all of the people]:

1. What is the clear purpose statement of what we, [all of us], are seeking to accomplish?
2. How well are we doing it?

Successful congregations have a clear, strong sense of purpose, around which they center their whole lives. Dynamic churches have these characteristics in common:

- They know where they are going.
- They have a clear plan for getting there.
- They [all] work wholeheartedly in unity to get the work done.

Spirit-directed purpose functions as a GPS or goggle map giving the individual believers and the church direction, general stability and balance no matter which direction the conditions of life may turn them:

- Integrating church life into consistent unity
- Providing a driving power and
- A compelling urgency

God is purposeful and moves toward consistent objectives. Of all His creatures, the human being is most like God in His ability to set goals and intelligently pursue them. The Biblical view of history is an intelligent, deliberate movement toward precise goals in the fulfillment of God's kingdom purpose.

Biblical Examples

Jesus' life was completely transparent because of His single-minded pursuit of a precise objective:

- He must be about His Father's business (Luke 2:49).
- For the Son of Man came to seek and to save that which was lost (Luke 19:10).
- My food is to do the will of Him who sent Me and to finish His work (John 4:34).

When Jesus' purpose was threatened by the king, Jesus sent His word, *"Go tell that fox,* 'I will cast out demons and heal people today and tomorrow, and on the third day I will reach My goal" (see Luke 13:32).

Because Jesus maintained His *single-minded commitment* to a clear purpose:

- He drove-off every opposing friend or foe.
- He maintained His own timetable.

- He could avoid unproductive activity and channel His entire life toward reaching its precise target, by death in the finishing of His work.
- His followers shared this quality.

The apostle Paul showed this totally focused life in Philippians 1:27-2:2:

"Only let your conduct be worthy of the gospel of Christ, so that whether I come and see you or am absent, I may hear of your affairs, that you stand fast in one spirit, with one mind striving together for the faith of the gospel, and not in any way terrified by your adversaries, which is to them a proof of perdition, but to you of salvation, and that from God. For to you it has been granted on behalf of Christ, not only to believe in Him, but also to suffer for His sake, having the same conflict which you saw in me and now hear is in me. Therefore if there is any consolation in Christ, if any comfort of love, if any fellowship of the Spirit, if any affection and mercy, fulfill my joy by being like-minded, having the same love, being of one accord, of one mind."

The student is no greater than his or her teacher. Christ is not only our Teacher, but also our Example. Church is Christ's idea, so His priority of goals must become ours. Otherwise we are trying to work His plan without Him. Paul wanted to cut a new path for the Philippians to follow to victory – the increasing of their faith would result in the increasing of their joy.

He may have said, "… that your rejoicing may be more abundant in Jesus Christ for me." Circumstances may cause us to lose our joy, but people can also bring trials that rob us of joy. How many times do we lose our peace and joy because of what people say and do?

The best remedy for these trials is a humble and single mind of purpose that seeks to honor Christ! Pride is the cause of much unrest and contention in the church (carefully study James 4), but genuine humility brings peace and joy. In other words, Paul lived on fruitfully, knowing that their joy and confidence would overflow because of Christ's working in him, not because of anything he himself did by his own ability.

Believers are to have integrity and live consistently what they believe, teach, and preach. This is in line with Paul's theme of unity of heart and one mind with the Philippians.

This task includes all the people, not just the "faithful few." He appealed to them on the basis of their Christian experience to have unity of mind and heart and to put others ahead of themselves.

The effective church is a *body of people* who have been "determined by one divine purpose.

It is captivated by Christ's mission. His purpose functions as the church's mission. Such a church has all the characteristics of a model's model. An early Christian document known as the letter to Diognrtus describes Christ's people in this way:

Christians cannot be distinguished from the rest of the human race by country or language or customs. They do not live in cities of their own; they do not use a peculiar form of speech; they do not follow an eccentric manner of life. This doctrine of theirs has not been discovered by the ingenuity of deep thought of inquisitive men, nor do they put forward merely human teaching, as some people do.

Yet although they live in Greek and barbarian cities alike, as each man's lot has been cast, and follows the customs of the country in clothing and food and other matters of daily living, at the same time they give proof of the remarkable and admittedly extraordinarily constitution of their own. They live in their own countries, but as aliens only.

They have a share in everything as citizens, and endure everything as foreigners. Every foreign land is their fatherland, and yet for them every fatherland is a foreign land........... It is true that they are "in the flesh," but they do not live "according to the flesh." They busy themselves on earth, but their citizenship is in heaven. They obey the established laws, but in their own lives they go far beyond what the laws require.[6] To God is the glory!

SUMMARY: CHAPTER 1

1. A church is effective so long as it single-mindedly pursues the purpose God has ordained for it.
2. From our study list several characteristics of a dynamic church.
3. Jesus' life was completely transparent because of His single-minded pursuit of a precise objective.
4. Believers are to have integrity and live consistently what they believe, teach and preach.
5. Discuss the negative effects caused by pride in the church.

CHAPTER TWO

IN HARMONY WITH REALITY

Then God said, *"Let us make man in Our image, according to Our likeness; let them have dominion over the fish of the sea, over the birds of the air, and over the cattle, over all the earth and over every creeping thing that creeps on the earth. So God created man in His own image; in the image of God He created him, male and female He created them"* (see Genesis 1:26-28).

Every church or Para-ministry has a philosophy of ministry to which they think or operate. It may be consistent or filled with contradictions, true or false, clear or cloudy. However, that philosophy provides a conceptual blueprint that reflects the purpose of how things ought to be, and how things really are; a diagram of views, assumptions, and convictions that provide direction. It is the standard by which ideas are tested.

Actions grow out of our operating value system – what we really believe; and our deepest convictions. However, it is possible to espouse one philosophy and operate by another. For example:

- Many of our local churches verbalize a biblical world view philosophy, but actually operate out of a philosophy based on institutional traditions of men, politics and favoritism.
- To be effective we must possess an integrity in which practice conforms to ideals.

A high level of effective church life and achievement happens when its leaders and members reach a consistently clear understanding of God's purpose for the church from [where it is] to [where it ought to be] and an accurate philosophy of ministry that is held in common; and guides the corporate effort.

_____ "where God wants the church to be"_____

The leadership must help the church to move from "where it is" to "where God wants it to be" today in [His purpose].

_____ "where the church is" _____

Again, all of the people must be clear and unified on such questions as:

- What are we as the church?
- Why are we here?
- Where are we going?
- How can we get from here to where we are going?
- How should we operate?

This is a key concept to which the apostle Paul called the Christian churches in Colossae and [the church worldwide] today as well:

"For this reason we also, since the day we heard it, do not cease to pray for you, and to ask that you may be filled with the knowledge of His will in all wisdom and spiritual understanding; that you may walk worthy of the Lord, fully pleasing Him, being fruitful in every good work and increasing in the knowledge of God; strengthened with all might, according to His glorious power, for all patience and longsuffering with joy; giving thanks to the Father who has qualified us to be partakers of the inheritance of the saints in the light. He has delivered us from the power of darkness and conveyed us into the

kingdom of the Son of His love, in whom we have redemption through His blood, the forgiveness of sins" (Colossians 1:9-14).

CREATION TO RECREATION AND THE CHURCH

God created the human being, designing it to function according to His principles and certain relationships in accordance with creation, other humans, and with God Himself. He desired a response from man that would be a voluntary, freely chosen, corporative relationship of trust and obedience. The man functioned according to design in harmony with reality (see Genesis 1, 2).

Satan opposed God with intentions of his own for humanity which comprised of contrary purposes, values, and standards for living that are in direct opposition. He engaged man in a relationship of manipulation, deception, and bondage (see Genesis 3).

The first man [Adam] chose Satan's alternatives to God's plan for man. His life was ejected from its creation design sending him into a state of tension and discord with God's principles which were structured in creation. Thus sin resulted in:

1. Man's alienation from God
2. Man's guilt
3. Disharmony with reality
4. Confused values and purposes
5. Frustration for women in labor
6. Pain and death

Further results from this original sin:

- The rest of creation was thrown out of alignment (see Genesis 3:17, 18; Romans 8:19-22).
- Satan [for a season] became the prince of this world (see John 12:31, 14:30).
- Human beings since that time by birth are made partakers of diseases and death (see Romans 5:12-14).
- Choosing Satan's *counter* principles for life; which are deeply embedded in the world's values and ways (see Romans 6:23; Galatians 3:22).

- We became spiritually distorted; resulting in alienation from God.

God's plan from the beginning

God created human life, designing it to function according to certain principles and to occupy certain relationships with others and with Him. However, Satan engaged God in a gigantic struggle for man's allegiance. Therefore, from the very beginning God had a plan to restore everything to His originally intended state without violating His own principles for interacting with mankind (Ephesians 1:3-14; 3:9-12; Acts 3:21).

- Jesus as the second Adam (1 Corinthians 15:45), entered the kingdom of the world.
- The purpose of God in Jesus was to *redeem man,* not *condemn him* and reestablish life as He *intended* it (John 3:14-21; 1:4, 5; 14:6).
- Jesus, the Redeemer, gave His life a sacrifice to reconcile man back to God and to remove the condemnation of sin (2 Corinthians 5:19; Colossians 1:20; Romans 5:6, 12-19; 6:22; 1 Timothy 1:15; 1 Peter 3:18).
- Through Jesus man is ushered into the grace of God and therefore restored to the proper relationship with Him (Ephesians 3:19).
- His resurrection validated His sacrifice and established Him as Lord.
- Additionally, Jesus *reinstituted* God's purposes, values, and principles of conduct for life (2 Timothy 1:9; Colossians 3:1 – 4:6).
- He not only *revealed* but also *demonstrated* the way life was designed to work.
- By committing themselves to Jesus as their Savior – His followers are reconciled to God.
- By committing themselves to Him as Lord, they are introduced to a way of life that is in harmony with principles rooted in the foundations of the world.

We must remember, as stated in an earlier section, methods change, but principles remain the same.

The Christian Community

Lest we forget, the Christian way of thinking and acting does not match the so-called "secular" patterns of life. The authentic Christian life is first of all supernatural [spiritual life], radical, and revolutionary – impossible to be properly lived in the flesh. The Christian *commits* himself or herself to:

- Live-out the details of this way of life by faith confident that they are true.
- Implements the ways revealed by Jesus even when they run counter to his or her ways.
- Distrusts and rejects the world's principles, values, and moral standards even when they seem right.
- Accepts the way of Christ as the one right way.

Our lives must be in proper alignment to spiritual reality if we are going to be meaningful – if our lives are to work. Christianity is God's adjuster. As the Christian incorporates God's truths his or her life is progressively transformed to function as God first intended. Ways of thinking and acting are renewed from the conformity of the world to the perfect will of God (see Romans 12:2).

Becoming a Christian is more than reform or simply adding religion to life; this process is so complete that Jesus called it being "born again" (see John 3:3) and entering a new kind of existence (2 Corinthians 5:17).

When people convert to Jesus Christ as they are pricked in their hearts upon hearing, repenting, and receiving the gospel by responding in obedience -- corporately these people are the church.

Spiritual growth and communal life

We can learn much about spiritual growth and communal life from Jesus' practice of small group life with the twelve disciples as a standard model to be replicated by the churches today. They did a lot together:

- Eating
- Traveling
- Teaching
- Healing

- Praying
- Listening
- Failing

The disciples did much of life together as they observed the Master's interaction with people as they sat under His teaching. Though you might have less time with your church small group; or you might meet only a few times a month the key is to become a community together for spiritual growth:

- Bible Study groups
- Prayer times together
- Community service together
- Worship
- Aiding group members in time of need and care

Perhaps not everyone will be at every gathering, but as long as members are connecting throughout the week – by phone, by email, text, chatting after a service – you will see the level of spiritual and communal growth increase tremendously.

It was natural therefore, for Jesus to develop a community of followers and for Paul, Peter, and other church planters [including us here at Bread of Life Ministries] to plant new communities; that began as small groups, just as Jesus had modeled with the twelve disciples:

And He went up on the mountain and called to Him those He Himself wanted. And they came to Him. Then He appointed twelve, that they might be with Him and that He might send them out to preach (Luke 3:13-14).

So they went out and preached that people might repent. And they cast out many demons, and anointed with oil many who were sick, and healed them (Luke 6:12-13; also see vv. 14-19).

Communal-focused groups were and integral part of the early church strategy. They were small enough to allow members to minister to *one another*, using their spiritual gifts to *mature* in the teachings of Christ. They were anointed and life-giving communities where *evangelism* and *service*[7] could take place as the unsaved watched a loving and compassionate community in action. Small group ministry created a sense of *oneness* while at the same time reaching out to a *lost* world for Christ.

These groups devoted themselves to the apostles teaching, to fellowship with one another, to practicing the Lord's Supper together and praying for one another. The Scriptures show that these communities were characterized by mutuality, accountability, service, love and evangelism. One pagan was noted to have expressed concerning those Christians, "O how they love one another!"

Dr. Francis Schaffer was one of the most influential Christian thinkers of the twentieth century. One of his most prominent theses was that, the way Christians interacted with one another, would be the final apologetic for whether or not non-Christians believed the gospel message.

Jesus said, *"A new commandment I give to you, that you love one another. By this all people will know that you are My disciples, if you have love for one another"* (John 13:34-35).

In his book *The Mark of a Christian* Schaffer reflected on this idea that he stated concerning the non-Christian in reference to Christ's statements in the verses above:

"Yet, without true Christians loving one another, Christ says the world cannot be expected to listen, even when we give proper answers. Let us be careful indeed, to spend a lifetime studying to give honest answers. For years the Orthodox Church has done this very poorly. So it is well to spend time learning to answer the questions of men who are about us. But after we have done our best to communicate to a lost world, still we must never forget the final apologetic which Jesus gives is the observable love of true Christians for true Christians." [8]

CHAPTER 2 REVIEW: HARMONY WITH RELITY

1. Discuss using the philosophy of ministry as a blueprint.
2. Discuss Paul's challenge to the Church (Colossians 1:9-14).
3. God desired a response from man (Adam) that would be a voluntary, freely chosen, corporative relationship out of trust and obedience.
4. Discuss several advantages of small group ministry.
5. What part does evangelism and witnessing play in the making of a disciple?

CHAPTER THREE

TWO KINGDOMS

"Enter by the narrow gate; for wide is the gate and broad is the way that leads to destruction, and there are many who go in by it. Because narrow is the gate and difficult is the way which leads to life, and there are few who find it" (Matthew 7:13-14).

Presently, there are two kingdoms in the world: one in which Satan and his way prevails, the other in which Jesus Christ is Lord and God's way prevails. Throughout the teachings of Jesus these two kingdoms are dominant themes:

- The two roads (see Matthew 7:13, 14)
- The wheat and the tares (see Matthew 13:24-30)
- The separation of fish (see Matthew 47-50)
- The two masters (see Matthew 6:24)

As the world moves farther and farther away from the Word and ways of God; which is the present trend, the distinctiveness of the children of God intensifies. In spite of the thinking of many in the secular community, the church is not a variation of the world. The church is a colony of the kingdom of God imbedded in the world. Christianity and the world represent two entirely different systems of life:

The Church	The World
Reconciled	Alienated
Truth	Error
Understanding	Confusion
Citizen with God	Alien to God
Alien to the world	Citizen of the world
Hope	Without hope
Saved	Lost
In light	In darkness
Wholeness	Brokenness
Mind of the Christ	Mind of the flesh, world
Life	Death
Free in Christ	Bondage
Ways of God	Ways of the world, Satan
Obedient	Disobedient
Peace with God	Enmity with God

CHRIST'S VICTORY

The Lord Jesus Christ in conquering Satan and his hosts has made possible complete victory for every believer. He is Lord over all principalities and powers. Satan has been stripped of his authority and Christ is dividing His spoil with the Church (see Luke 11:20-22; Psalm 19:5; Isaiah 53:12). This victory of Christ is seen in three segments: in His life, in His death and in His resurrection:

In His sinless Life

Jesus was tempted in the wilderness in the three areas of human's being: spirit, soul, and body and in the three areas of sin: the lust of the flesh, the lust of the eyes, and the pride of life (see Matthew 4:11; Luke

4:1-13; 1 Thessalonians 5:23; I John 2:15-16). As the last Adam and the second man, He was submitted to the attacks and temptations of Satan and proved His complete victory over him.

- Satan had tempted the first Adam in these areas (Genesis 3:1-6). The first Adam fell, thus bringing his entire future race under satanic control and into his kingdom of sin, darkness, and death.
- In the wilderness Satan sought to gain dominion over the last Adam, Jesus Christ. He was tempted:

1. Body – the lust of the flesh (Luke 4:2-4)
2. Soul – the lust of the eyes (Luke 4:5-8)
3. Spirit – the pride of life (Luke 4:9-2)

The Scripture says, He [Jesus] was tempted in all points like as we are, yet without sin (see Hebrews 2:18; 4:18). Though the first Adam was defeated by Satan – the last Adam was victorious. He overcame [Satan] by the Word of God.

It was necessary for Jesus Christ to win His personal victory over Satan before He could gain a representative victory for all believers. Christ's power during His earthly life over sin, sickness, demons and death was founded on the three-fold victory over temptation. Having conquered the devil for Himself – He could conquer him for His people. He is also now the Head of the new creation race. Give Him praise and glory!

In His Substitutionary Death

Christ's victory in the wilderness temptation was in *His* own behalf. The victory on Calvary's cross was in *our* behalf. This victory was actually begun in Gethsemane (see Luke 22:53) and consummated on the Cross (see Colossians 2:14-15; John 12:31; 16:11). In the cross He defeated the principalities and powers, and made a show of them, triumphing over them in it.

In His Resurrection and Ascension

Christ's victory over Satan in the wilderness involved His *personal* victory, and Calvary His *representative* victory, it also includes His victory which is to be manifest in the heavenly realms (see Luke 10:18; Job 1:6-12; 2:1-7; Revelation 12:9-12; Colossians 2:10; Ephesians 1:19-23; 2:2; Hebrews 4:12-14).

As believers we can rejoice in Christ's full and complete victory over Satan's entire *kingdom of darkness*. All are subject to Him. God has given Christ to be Head over all things to the Church. What Christ did on Calvary was for God, and for His Church.

THE MINISTRY OF THE CHURCH

Involved in the purpose of God for the Church is that which is spoken of in Ephesians 3:10-11, *"To the intent that now unto the manifold wisdom of God might be made known by the church to the principalities and powers in the heavenly places.' according to the eternal purpose which He accomplished in Christ Jesus our Lord.*

God's plan for the redemption of man includes the use of the Church, Christ's body, to also subdue Satan. Christ has delegated His authority to the Church corporately and to believers individually (see Mark 9:38-39; 16:15-20; Acts 19:13-18; Matthew 24:14; Luke 22:26-30).

When you study the history of the early Church in the Book of Acts, you find that as men and women came to the Savior, as stated earlier, they immediately banded themselves together in small groups to form churches. They worshiped God and had a ministry of "strengthening the disciples and encouraging them to remain true to the faith" (see Acts 14:22).

To proclaim the gospel of the kingdom is to teach and preach the truth of God's Word, heal the sick and cast out demons. The Great Commission includes the preaching of the Gospel with signs following. In the Great Commandment and Great Commission the Lord was commissioning the Church, which is His Body, to continue His ministry on earth (see Acts 1:1, 8; Luke 4:18-20; Acts 26:18; Matthew 28:19-20; Luke 24:47-49). The Book of Acts demonstrates the power of the Gospel – proclaimed on the basis of Christ's finished work.

To attend church is to be part of a local assembly of believers, which is the local manifestation of the body of Christ universal. The writer to the Hebrews *warned* his generation about forsaking the gathering together of the Church of Jesus Christ (see Hebrews 10:24-25).

To turn from darkness to light

Christ has given the Church a power of attorney, the right to use His Name and continue His ministry on earth. The ministry of the Church could be concluded in the Lord's commission to the Apostle Paul in Acts 26:18,

"To open their eyes, and to turn them from darkness to light, and from the power of Satan unto God, that they may receive forgiveness of sins, and inheritance among them which are sanctified by faith that is in Me."

To "turn from darkness to light" refers to "repentance" which includes a complete change of mind and thinking. For some ungodly reason churches are not emphasizing "repentance" as an essential part of the salvation experience. In spite of what Jesus said,

"I tell you, no;
but unless you
repent
you will all
likewise perish"
– Luke 13:5

The event referred to here in the text was a natural tragedy as opposed to the violent human act alluded to in vv. 1, 2. However, the same question was asked; were the people who died being judged for their sins? Even today this question comes up when a saint dies a violent or horrendous death. The manner in which a person dies is not a measure of their righteousness. What is most important is *not to die* outside of God's grace and mercy. Again, the way to avoid such a fate is to **repent,** to come to God through the loving care of the Great Physician, Jesus Christ. Jesus' mission was to call sinners to repentance. Upon His ascension, Jesus commissioned His disciples to the same task:

Jesus said, *"I came not to call the righteous, but sinners to **repentance.***

Then He said to them, *"Thus it is written, and thus it was necessary for the Christ to suffer and to rise from the dead the third day, and that **repentance*** *and **remission** of sins should be preached in His name to all nations, beginning at Jerusalem"* (Luke 24:46-47).

The focus of the disciples preaching would center on God's gracious offer of forgiveness to all who believe – that mission has not changed; our task today is the same (study carefully Acts 2:30-39).

One of the greatest examples of repentance can be seen in the life of the apostle Paul. In Romans 12:2, he speaks of the "renewing of your mind." We do what we think is best; what makes sense to us. Paul who was formerly named Saul; a Pharisee was killing Christians, because he thought it was the right course of action. Christ's revelation changed his thoughts and he became the apostles to the Gentiles. His preaching of the Good News was *visible proof* that he had *repented* from his past ways. Genuine repentance is evidenced by our changed behavior.

The goal of evangelism

Many times, the thing a person says before he or she leaves is the most important thing to remember. While the disciples stood on the Mount of Olives, as Jesus was soon to depart, they must have realized that they were *experiencing* a life-changing moment. What Jesus was saying was very important. From this point on, they have one word to define who they are. They were *"witnesses."*

Several terms are used in Scripture to describe the process of evangelism. Evangelism is "communicating *the gospel* in an understandable manner and motivating the individual to receive Christ and become a responsible and maturing member of His Church." There is a personal fulfillment and inner joy when you *effectively* share your faith with other people that cannot be *experienced* any other manner. God's goal for the church is for "all" [100%] of us to be involved in evangelism.

Please remember, a goal without a plan – is just a wish!

Too often in our estimation, we define effective evangelism according to our stereotyped pictures of an evangelistic ministry. Real effective evangelism's key is definitely not found in a *program* but rather a *person*, who shares his or her faith out of the overflow of their righteous life.

To prevent the stereotypes, and those who offer excuses for not participating, Jesus made us all *witnesses,* to make sure the world is evangelized. Therefore no generation would ever be ignorant of *"the wonderful works of God"* (see Acts 2:11).

With such an important *responsibility* in our hands – we must do all we can to be a credible *witness* everywhere we go. The most effective people who witness are those who develop a credible lifestyle and conversation. The Bible has much to say about the kind of person who is effective in evangelism:

- The most effective witness flows out of a maturing development of spiritual concern for others. This person faithfully shares his or her faith with those who do not know Christ as Savior (see Psalms 126:6; Romans 9:1-3; 10:1).

- Many Christians are effective in sharing their faith because they love the Lord. When people do things for love they have more passion. Understanding just how much God loves us, allows us to naturally share His love with others (see 1 John 4:9, 19; Romans 5:5; II Corinthians 5:14).

- God's love in our hearts makes us willing to serve others even when no one expects it (see I Corinthians 9:19).

- Effective believers witness in the power of the Holy Spirit and the gospel making a positive difference in the lives of others (see Romans 1:16).

- Truly born again people who are now new creations "in Christ" (2 Corinthians 5:17) are more likely to recognize the life-changing potential of the gospel in the lives of others (1 Timothy 1:12-15).

There's an old saying, "I'd rather see a sermon any day than hear one. People tend to listen to a witness when they have seen a positive difference in his or her lifestyle; especially when they see how they handle problems. Peter reminded Christians to be prepared in the midst of suffering to explain the gospel to anyone who asks (see I Peter 3:14-17).

Those people matured in the faith exercises wisdom in approaching people to talk about salvation; they have a special empowerment from the Lord (see Proverbs 11:30; James 1:5). Additionally, when we make personal Bible study an on-going spiritual discipline in our daily lives, God gives us wisdom (Psalm 19:7).

God has taken a great risk, by entrusting us with the responsibility to take the gospel to the whole world – to partner with the Spirit and the Word of God working in tandem as others come to faith in Jesus Christ; which results in much glory to God.

Essential preparation for witnessing

Authentic witnessing in evangelism is done in the power of the Holy Spirit. In Ephesians 5:18, all believers are commanded to *"Be filled with the Spirit."* In the New Testament, being filled with the Spirit is the consistent evidence of the power for evangelism (Acts 1:8). How do we obtain this power?

- By desiring to be filled with the Holy Spirit
- Repenting of known sin in our lives
- Receiving the fullness of the Spirit through prayer
- Trusting God to fill us and use us

– John 7:37-39

The same Spirit who empowers us to be effective in witnessing:

- Also empowered the Bible to be effective in the salvation of people (see 2 Timothy 3:15).
- The "Word of Life," another biblical phrase used for the Word of God that produces the spiritual life in others (see Philippians 2:16).

Often Christians try to do evangelism in their own strength rather than relying upon the power of the Holy Spirit. While there may be some minimal success, doing evangelism [witnessing]; but witnessing in the full power of the Holy Spirit results in greater effectiveness and certainly the success that God intended.

CHAPTER 3 REVIEW [TWO KINGDOMS]

1. Discuss the church as a colony of the kingdom of God.
2. Christianity and the world represent two entirely different systems of life.
3. What was Satan's objective in the wilderness with the second Adam, Jesus Christ?
4. To proclaim the gospel of the kingdom is to teach, and preach the truth of God's Word and heal the sick.
5. Discuss the power of attorney that Jesus gave to His Church.

CHAPTER FOUR

THE DIVINE STRATEGY

"Walk worthy of the calling with which you were called, with all lowliness, and gentleness, with longsuffering, bearing with one another in love, endeavoring to keep the unity of the Spirit in the bond of peace. There is one body and one Spirit, just as you were called in one hope of your calling" (Ephesians 4:1-4).

It would be unthinkable to go into battle without first training and equipping your soldiers with adequate plans, appropriate provisions, and weaponry for expected victory. Before the foundation of the world God considered what resources His army [the Body of Christ], universal would need to survive and fully function among Satan's tares strewn among them from Pentecost to the Rapture of the Church.

Study after study has shown that the present crisis among many local churches is caused in part by the lack of a strategy geared toward moving the church forward. In fact in many cases they have no plans for bringing their believers into maturity and Christlikeness; or carrying out the Great Commission.

Therefore, their unspoken strategy is to just maintain the "status quo" by continuing to meet for their own *traditional* version of:

- spiritual enrichment and in-house programming;
- totally oblivious of the lost world outside around them.

GOD'S DIVINE STRATEGY

Therefore if we expect God's divine strategy through necessary *change* to occur in people's lives, the community life of the church must be central, and the epicenter of both the work of the Spirit and the transformational power of the Word.

This strategy is a dynamic, purpose-oriented equipping concept. It means to, "adequately furnish or prepare someone for service or action." Notice the same term is also used in Ephesians 6:10-18, where the apostle Paul describes the Christian becoming fully armed and outfitted for spiritual warfare (carefully study Ephesians 6).

When the Spirit works through us, He anoints and blesses our words, and our works. These works may be small in the estimation of others, but their impact is like the ripples we see when we toss a stone into a pond. The stone-caused ripples expand through time in increasingly wide circles until it reaches the other shore. When we:

- complete a godly assignment
- speak a word in love
- pray for a brother or sister
- properly train up a child
- distribute a Bible or other equipping materials
- share a testimony
- teach a one on one lesson or a group
- give generously in support of a ministry
- support other Christian workers

We never know the chain reaction God will strategically begin. We can't begin to imagine the cumulative effect of our simple acts of service, influence or word. That's why the Bible says, "Let us not grow weary while doing good, for in due season we shall reap if we do not lose heart" (see Galatians 6:9).

We are frequently reminded in the Word, of God's method of multiplication [His divine strategy] principle of sowing and reaping. A single seed has the power or capacity within to reproduce the necessary harvest to feed millions. The story is told of a man holding an acorn in his hand and asking three young boys what they saw in it: The first boy said he saw an acorn. The second said he saw an oak tree. The third boy excitedly exclaimed, "I see a whole forest of oak trees!"

As Children of God, we go through life sowing words, deeds, and our influence – some no larger than a mustard seed. But the number of people Christ can influence through us is incalculable. Now that is God's math – He created mathematics.

The world is not random; it is well ordered with His unchangeable mathematical equations that are constant and absolute. Notice how God deals in higher powers:

- At the beginning of our education, we learned the numbers one through ten. Add them up and you'll get 55.
- Now multiply them: $1x2x3x4x5x6x7x8x9x10 == 3,628,800$.

God knows how to turn our addition into His multiplication. Perhaps we can find our proper niche by reviewing the words add and multiply in the Book of Acts:

In the first chapters we see additions used:

"Those who accepted his message were baptized, and about three thousand were added to their number that day" (Acts 2:21).

"And the Lord added to their number daily those who were being saved" (Acts 2:47).

"More and more men and women believed in the Lord and were added to their number" (Acts 5:14).

Beginning in the next chapter, Acts 6 the word changes from addition to multiplication:

"The number of the disciples was multiplying" (Acts 6:1).

"The Word of God, spread, and the number of disciples multiplied greatly" (Acts 6:7).

"Then the churches throughout all Judea, Galilee, and Samaria ….. were multiplied"(Acts 9:31).
We can begin by:

1. Inviting unsaved people to become part of Christ's church and movement.
2. Once they are saved, He or she works to enable other Christians to achieve God's purpose.

Equipping is the mutual assignment and responsibility of every member in the body of Christ. Ephesians 4:11-13 has become the focal point for decades in clarifying the roles of church leaders and Christian workers [all are New Testament priests].

The word in verse twelve often translated "perfecting" contains the idea of preparing someone for a job. In God's design for church leaders; their task is not to do the work of the kingdom on the behalf of other Christians, but it is to equip others to do the work of the kingdom.

The minister shares in his or her special role assisting others in the ministry to become more fully equipped. The Christian who receives the instructions and training *must transmit to others* what he or she has received. In the Biblical model the Lord instructed Paul; and he in turn instructed Timothy and directed him to entrust this to "other faithful men [and women] who will also be equipped to teach others (see 2 Timothy 2:2).

An equipping ministry

Much of the explanation for the confusion that exists so widely in many of our local churches today is that – Christians have been looking at the things seen *instead* of at the things that are not seen. We see a suffering world full of groaning and screaming people everywhere; as hatred, bigotry, misery and injustice increase at an astronomical rate.

Everyone is nervous, "What are we going to do?" "Let's do something if it's wrong!" Don't these comments sound logical? Many churches and individual Christians only see things that are visible. As King Solomon put it, "things under the sun." We apply shallow human remedies to the situation and it grows worse – we wonder why.

Christ has given the authority to the entire body of Christ, "in His name," yet sadly, the potential for spiritual power and achievement remains unexplored for most Christians and churches. It seems that most congregations are satisfied to operate within their own human parameters [science, reason and experience].

Congregations operating in human abilities demonstrate a low level of accomplishment – operating routinely on such level of what is "possible," "practical," "realistic," and "desirable," whatever is accomplished is done using human wisdom, human resources, human ingenuity, and human effort alone. The people plan, make decisions, and operate as if all were up to them. They act as if no potential outside them exists, as if God is out there somewhere, but not a part of the present time and place. Some have referred to this attitude as "practical humanism," constantly speaking words about the power of the Holy Spirit and the Word, but never seeking or acting on the truth and power available through the indwelling Spirit.

One person observed, "If God ever went out of business, some churches would never know the difference." Well, God will not ever go out of business [His business], when He raptures the Church many individuals and many local churches will try to continue in some form probably without a clue as to what happened, [all those people gone!]. This reminds me of my first car, a 1949 Chrysler [passed down from soldier to soldier as he left going back to the States], I purchased it in France for $50 in 1961. The starter was inoperable and the transmission would not shift into reverse gear, so to get from point A to point B, I had to have many friends to help push-start it or if I was alone; always parked on a hill and never parked in places where reverse gear was required. Parts for American cars were non-existent in those days; so you find something to make it work. Some would probably say, that walking or riding a bus would have been more feasible. I guess that's the conclusion many Christians are making concerning the way we do church today.

Many of our local churches have acquired so many entertaining add-ons and so much religious dead weight that consciously or unconsciously they have moved away from God's purpose and strategy altogether. In fact for many the Holy Spirit has no place because, as so many pastors put it, "His presence makes many people *feel* uncomfortable and they won't come back." What many are doing is make do? God forbid!

Eighteen years ago my wife and I planted the Bread of Life, a Para ministry, for the purpose equipping the saints to do the work of ministry." At that time (1998), a Barna report noted 20 million Christians who had dropped out of the traditional and institutional churches, and were not joined to another. Over the years we have established eight schools with this mission of equipping the saints to do the work of ministry. Every place we've established a school, we in turn have planted a Bible-believing – Bible-teaching Church. Though located in several States the mission is the same. People are hungry for the *truth* of God's Word.

A recent 2016 report indicated that number has increased to 117 million unchurched spiritually alive Christians many of whom feel that their church experience is doing them and their families more harm than good. This does not mean they are no longer Christians, but they are seeking a simpler more Bible-believing and Christ-like life of righteousness. A growing number of those fleeing are from the Traditional and Institutional Black Churches. Many of those in this migration are joining or planting house churches or storefront churches both of which are flourishing and multiplying in numbers. Others are joining white congregations. Sadly, this whole situation has opened the door for a vast number of hirelings and people with little or no church or ministerial training to enter.

After thirty years as a pastor, I contend that among the reasons for the large decline in our churches can be attributed to:

- Rejection of the truth of Gods Word.
- The churches' choice of experience, science, and reason for authority and guidance over the Holy Spirit and His ministries.
- Model good-citizenship over Christlikeness.
- Many churches have lost the gospel of salvation.
- The seven last words of a dying church – "We have never done it like that!"

Additionally, the millennia find such churches boring and irrelevant to their needs. Many of these lifeless churches are all that these young people have known or have been exposed to from birth. Therefore, once they leave home, they also leave the church. In fact many local churches have not been exposed to the Holy Spirit with His gifts and ministries, mainly because to do so would put many church leaders' power in jeopardy due to the abolishment of the traditions of men.

Church history reflects that the Holy Spirit was absent from the church for 1100 years at which time the Roman Catholic Church was the depository of Christianity. However the purity of the Word of God was preserved in the Monastic communities during that long period. In 1906 a black preacher, William Seymour traveled from Houston, Texas to Los Angeles to preach a week of revival services in a black holiness church, Mrs. Julia Hutchins was the pastor. When he preached his first sermon, proclaiming that "speaking in tongues" was the "initial evidence" of one's receiving the baptism in the Holy Spirit, he caused quit a stir and flurry of activities.

Though locked out of the church that night, Seymour did not leave the city but continued to preach the "new" so-called theory thus stated; and soon the services began to flourish, and the ensuing revival lasted from 1906 – 1909. Many thriving denominations and churches such as: C. H. Mason and the Church of God in Christ, M.M. Pinson and H. G. Rodgers and the Assembles of God, G.B. Cashwell and the Pentecostal Holiness, and the Church of the Nazarene were born out of that revival which became internationally known as the *Pentecostal Movement.* From Azusa Street, the Pentecostal flame spread to Canada, across Europe, Central and South America, Russia and other Slavic nations.

Today, more than a hundred years after the 1906 Azuzu Street Revival, the denominational churches born out of that revival that retained the Pentecostal flame are among the fastest growing churches around the world.[9]

Biblically speaking, prior to this movement the church, [Roman Catholicism], was about dead works, a form of godliness that denied the power, [Holy Spirit and His ministries], thereof – they easily fell into the sin Jesus warned about; which is over-commitment to the self-serving affairs and a life of [promoting a salvation by dead works]. Undoubtedly much of this behavior carried over into the Reformation churches.

The fervor of the Pentecostal flame is still moving around the world. My wife and I have worked with these "fired-up" churches in North America, Central and South America, and the Republic of South Korea. While the speaking in tongues as the "initial evidence" still thrives in many churches, the ministry of the Holy Spirit has revealed many other spiritual gifts and graces of which "tongues" and "interpretation" are included for the building up of the church. The spiritual gifts have been moved across denominational lines as the Holy Spirit moves to cleanse and bring to Christlikeness, the true Church (the Bride of Christ) for the Rapture. Give God a shout of praise!

Satan knows his time is short

Unable to destroy God's creation, Satan has set out to contaminate it. Since Eden he has wrecked havoc on the planet. His foot prints can be seen in every newscast, in over crowded courts, and rebellion among people of all age groups. At 77 years of age, I can remember a much, much better America. Though he is trying his best, I don't envision Satan being able to totally destroy any of the institutions that God Himself has instituted.

In the news media and even at all levels of our secular-driven education systems secular humanists and atheists have been able to plant their evolution theory by indoctrinated people – with the intention of destroying God's creation truth. Today, June 8, 2017, on the national news a skull was held up and heralded as the oldest human skull ever discovered and scientists inferring it to be 300,000 years old. The oldest discovery prior was a skull estimated to be 100,000 years old.

When I was a student in Elementary School more than 60 years ago, we studied the *theory* of evolution, and though the theory has been elevated to so-called science today – proof wise it remains a theory, simply because requirements for classification as science are just not there. However, taking the Bible out of the schools has taken a toll on the students in fact; children educated over the past 20 years have been fully indoctrinated. While the home and the church were distracted by the culture, Satan's contamination has almost removed the Bible from them also, as secularism and multiculturalism are being widely accepted over Christianity. Their presence and influences are felt in many critical leadership roles across this nation. To the secularist things are measured "according to human*(ism)* thought;" which places human beings as the supreme measure of all things; since they do not believe in Creation or the God of Creation.

The origin of all history, the Holy Bible, announces the beginning of the heavens and the earth, and of plant, animal, and human life. The events recorded in Genesis cover a period of 2,315 years (Usher). Thus the recorded history of the beginning of the entire universe is found only in the Bible. Creation places human beings beginning at 6000 years old.

It has been said that children are the most loved and the most abused. This is certainly true when a comparison is made of children exposed to the teaching of Creation in the home. We can all see from this that we are raising a generation of children who are indoctrinated to believe the great lie, evolution!

One of the names given of the Holy Spirit in the gospel of John is "the Spirit of truth." Jesus promised, *"When He the Spirit of truth comes He will guide you into all truth"* (John 6:13).

The greatest example is in the creation of human beings. The Scripture *distinctly* says God created humans *male* and *female*. Satan has countered with a plan to neutralize or *distinctly* change God's gender order to *male* and *male;* and *female* and *female*. This very day the media is promoting his agenda with a story of a family of five: 1 husband [male] and 1 wife [female] with three teenaged daughters.

After two decades of marriage the mother *feels* that she really is a male in a female body so she has begun reassignment orientation which she claims places her into a position to help her teenaged daughter who is confused because she *feels* her gender is really male and she is also in the process of reassignment orientation.

The reporter praised the father, who through much counseling has come to accept the situation. The wife exclaiming that their marriage has been strengthened through the ordeal. This is the fruit of a *growing* secular society which is right on target with secular humanism's agenda, as outlined in their Manifesto.[10] Today this family could very well be members in a local Christian church.

The permissiveness of secularized thought is introduced in kindergarten and subtly promoted into grade schools, colleges and universities. It has been noted that graduate students from our institutions of higher learning for the pass twenty five years are thoroughly indoctrinated with evolution theory as the truth over biblical creation. Secularism humanism, atheism along with multiculturalism have dominated the culture and have respectfully made inroads into the local churches [but has not conquered by any means] the true Church of the Living God.

America has allowed something to happen that history reports to be devastating for any country; that is when the founding faith is removed or destroyed, so goes the country. Multiculturalism has deemed all faiths to be equal in the United States; therefore Christianity is no longer the dominant faith; as many of our local churches are assimilating portions the Eastern faiths and practices as their "yoga" and "meditation" have been adopted as part of the progressive church culture.

Additionally, the secular media fosters such scare tactics as placing "post" to every founding institution, morality, and authority, thus passing on the impression that they are no longer needed, antiquated, or not relevant – we hear "post Christian," "post modern," "post church," "post family" etc. A person who does not study the Bible is easily impressed with these claims even those in the church; in fact I would venture to say even many local churches have succumbed to secular culture through this deception as they replace the authority of the Scripture with the authority of the culture.

Churches dying today are not necessarily dying because they are traditional, independent or a particular denomination per say, but most are dying because of disobedience toward the Lord's commands of:

1. God's ultimate goal of Christlikeness for all believers.
2. Christ's command to "Go make disciples!"

Naturally we claim to love God and ourselves, but many Christians individually and corporately have forgotten or have never known the second part of the Great Commandment to "love your neighbor as yourself." "Do we really know who our neighbors are?" If we are having problems with the Great Commandment, certainly we will not be faithful at making disciples. Such selective disobedience further reflects the nation's growing spiritual and biblical deficiency.

Secular confusion

Secular Humanism places its total trust in science and intelligence rather than God's divine guidance – they don't believe in God or the supernatural.

Thus, secular humanists do not rely upon gods or other supernatural forces to solve their problems or to provide guidance for their conduct [which gives the church a tremendous advantage]. We have the victory in Jesus!

- They look solely upon the application of science, reason, technology, the lessons of history, and personal experience to form an ethical and moral foundation to create meaning in life.

- They look to the methodology of science as the most reliable source of information available about what is factual or true about the universe we all live in.

- Having said all of that, their problem-solving outlook draws primarily from human experience, reason, technological and medical science.

Secular humanism then is a philosophy or religion and world view which centers upon human concerns and employs rational and scientific methods to address the wide range of cultural issues important to us all. Soon rejection of the Christian's worldview will be so ingrained until people will automatically believe that Christians are the enemy whose only cure is isolation or assimilation. Those taking this suggested path must abandon God's divine strategy in order to be acceptable. Please keep in mind, secular humanism is at odds with faith-based religious systems and Christianity in particular on many issues.[11]

In recent years, atheists and humanists have become so well-placed in our society occupying powerful positions at all levels of family life, education, branches of government, and all professions of the marketplace in general that they no longer try to conceal their true interests, but openly acknowledging their beliefs.

I'm really convinced that they think it is too late for the pro-moral people of this country to boot them out of office or positions of public trust and influence. I don't agree with their assessment of the situation at all! I am convinced if we repent and turn back to God, our true Source for everything He will help us. We must be in communion with Christ, committed to obedience and application of God's Word. I was invited be the guest speaker some years ago at an Emancipation Proclamation service in one of our Southeastern cities. It was a great experience.

I was given the "key to the city." I prayed much, adhered to the time allotted and poured out my heart, after all I was asked to bring the sermon [preach], afterward the presiding officer came to the podium and said, "WOW!" He then shot me a few "Atta boys" and turned back to the microphones and said, "Oh! What Dr. Leach said in that message was so challenging ----"but!" Long ago I was told that the word "but" has the power to erase everything that came before it. Certainly I found that to be true that day. He being a State Senator went right back to political business as usual for them, but on the home-front many were challenged as the sermon struck a nerve and other doors were opened. Praise God!

We talk so much about red and blue States, Democrats and Republicans, Independents, liberals, conservatives, and un-affiliated, but never atheists and humanists which are not parties or religions per se, since humanism no longer classify itself as a religion; although it was classified as such in its beginning. The secular humanists are Republicans, Democrats, Independents and many of them are church members, [*standing in the shadows*], but all in support of an agenda geared; it seems to destroy this country. I will list several preambles and tenets from their Humanist Manifesto 2000 [A Call to a New Planetary Humanism]:

Preamble I: Humanism is an ethical, scientific and philosophical outlook that has changed the world. Its heritage traces back to the philosophers and poets of ancient Greece and Rome, Confucian China and the Charvaka movement in classical India. Humanist artists, writers, scientists and thinkers have been shaping the modern era for over half a millennium.

Indeed, humanism and modernism have often seemed synonymous for humanist ideas and values express a renewed confidence in the power of human beings to solve their own problems and conquer uncharted people on the planet.

Preamble II: Prospects for a better future. Advance happiness, and freedom, and enhance human life for all people on the planet.

Preamble VIII: A New Global Agenda. We will need to work increasingly with and through the new centers of power and influence to improve equity and stability, alleviate poverty, reduce conflict, and safeguard the environment.[12]

I say again! "The wicked shall be turned into hell and all nations that turn their backs on God" (Psalm 9:7).

It is important that every Christian knows the subtle ways that the secular agenda is manifesting itself all around us and undermining the true biblical worldview. Below are listed a number of tenets from the Secular Humanist Manifesto. The humanists:

- Do not believe that God exists and therefore man is the highest entity [the measuring standard of all things].
- Believe the Bible is the work of men alone.
- Believe evolution is the means to explain the existence of life.
- See man as basically good.
- Believe that some things are right for some people and even some situations that may be wrong for other people and other situations are right for them.
- Believe that there is no absolute right and wrong; everything depends on the situation.
- Believe this physical life is all there is, so their goal is to get as much happiness and gain as many things they can before time runs out and he or she ceases to exist.
- Believe that since man is merely a highly evolved animal, some human life is not special therefore secular humanism supports abortion, euthanasia, pedophilia, and even infanticide.
- Believe that since man is merely a highly evolved animal, sexual gratification is not to be denied as long as "it doesn't hurt anyone." We can see these people in the highest office – but now you understand the very lenient sentence for rape and even murder.
- Believe that since man is merely a highly evolved animal, no sexual acts should be considered improper so long as "it doesn't hurt anyone." How is that possible?
- View man as the supreme being of the universe.
- Reject the existence of God and the supernatural.
- See moral values as relative, changing and varying from person to person.
- Seeks to eradicate biblical Christianity.[13]

The Scripture says, *"See to it that no one takes you captive through philosophy and empty deception, according to the traditions of men, according to the elementary principles of the world, rather than according to Christ"* (Colossians 2:8 AMP).

Research shows that today's young people are caught up in atheism and secular humanism [they are prepped and oriented from K – High School] upon leaving home and church for college, the military, or secular careers, unlike past generations, they are not returning to church later in life. Unless they have a truly spiritual experience prior to leaving home, – atheism and secularism humanism awaits them in every arena of life to gobble them up!

"Be sober, be vigilant; because your adversary the devil walks about like a roaring lion, seeking whom he may devour" (1 Peter 5:8).

Like Paul, the apostle Peter warns the believer to be aware of our adversary, Satan our avowed enemy; then he passes on some spiritual counsel:

- Be *sober*, meaning to be self-disciplined, use common sense and do not think foolishly.

- Again, he warns be *vigilant*, meaning be alert to the *spiritual pitfalls* of life and take appropriate action to make certain we do not stumble.

- Satan never ceases his hostilities toward the children of God; and he is constantly accusing us before God (see Revelation 12:10; Luke 22:31).

I think we under estimate Satan who like a roaring lion is both cunning and cruel. Humanism began as a religion, but dropped out giving them a free-hand indoctrinating our children and at the same time rejecting and discrediting Christianity at every opportunity. Therefore, those Christians who support the atheistic and humanist agenda are under satanic control and either knowingly or unknowingly they prove to be [practical humanists]. He attacks when least expected and desires to destroy completely those in his sights. Brethren Satan will use anyone, and He is not your friend!

Resist him! We are not commanded to run from the devil, but to resist or fight rather than flee. Victory comes when we remain committed to God, no matter the situation – because greater is He that is in us than our enemy! John writes,

"You are of God, little children, and have overcome them, because He who is in you is greater than he who is in the world" (1 John 4:4).

Here John turns from the importance of love (3rd Chapter) to the importance of belief in the truth of God's Word. Once again he focuses on the doctrinal test and emphasizes the need to obey sound teaching (see Matthew 24:1; 2 Peter 2:2, 3; Jude 3). The Scripture presents sharp warnings against:

- False doctrine
- Temptations
- Satan's attempts to distort and deny God's Word (see Genesis 3:1-5).
- The demonic source behind all false teachers (2 Corinthians 11:13, 14).

As in John's day, Christians are to have a healthy skepticism concerning any teaching – unlike some in his congregations who were too open-minded to anyone claiming a new thing regarding "the faith" (see Jude 3). Believers are to be like the Bereans who, as students of the Word, searched the Scriptures to discern truth and error (Acts 17:11-12).

He emphasizes that they be able to discern whether the one behind human teachers who propagates the message is either a demon spirit or the Holy Spirit. True believers have nothing to fear, since those who have experienced the new birth have the indwelling Spirit who has built into us checks against false teaching:

But you have an anointing from the Holy One, and you know all things. I have not written to you because you do not know the truth, but because you know it, and that no lie is of the truth (I John 2:20).

But the anointing which you have received from Him abides in you, and you do not need that anyone teach you; but as the same anointing teaches you concerning all things, and is true, and is not a lie, and just as it has taught you, you will abide in Him (v. 27).

John is not denying the importance of gifted teachers in the church, but he points out that neither those teachers nor those believers are dependent on human wisdom or the opinions of any person for the truth. God's Holy Spirit guards and guides the true believer into the truth:

- The Holy Spirit leads the true Christian into sound doctrine; which evidences the new birth experience has taken place (see Romans 8:17).
- True believers do not have to fear Satan and his demons nor their perversions, because they cannot take them out of the Lord's hand. Praise God!

Here, as mentioned earlier is protection against error and victory over it is guaranteed by sound doctrine and the illumination of the Holy Spirit (see 1 John 2:18-27).

CHAPTER 4: REVIEW AN EQUIPPING STRATEGY

1. Why have so many churches thrown out or shelved the Great Commission?
2. According to 2 Timothy 2:2, what is the task of believers once they are qualified to teach?
3. Secular humanism is at odds with faith-based religious systems and Christianity.
4. Discuss the impact of secular humanism on education today.
5. Young people are not returning to church after college, military service or other careers. Ponder some of the reasons why?

SECTION II

WE ARE HERE

CHAPTER FIVE

GETTING A HANDLE ON REALITY

"Therefore let us pursue the things which make for peace and the things by which one may edify another" (Romans 14:19).

Children are a heritage of the Lord [most loved and most abused]. The ever increasing crime rates, decreases in meaningful church membership and attendance, coupled with cold love, spiritual and biblical illiteracy; many of this generation's young pastors probably feel cheated by prior generations. They are finding a generational gap in the church similar to the one outside. However, that ought to not be in the church. I pray some of our retiring pastors will help fill the gap with the needed generational leadership, counsel and guidance.

The very idea that the community they were raised up in no longer understands their frustrations, struggles and mindsets. Many in the present generation like prior generations are looking down their noses at their elders. However, when the elders maintain their proficiency and remain committed to the mission; the young people will flock to them so the elders can pour into them our love, wisdom and knowledge of the faith and life.

I have often wondered why so many of my nearest friends are little more than half my age – however over time I knew what they were after. At 77 years of age, I continue to pastor, teach in the Bible College, write and publish one or two books a year. My wife and I have been sought out for preaching, teaching workshops, seminars and speaking engagements without let up for years. God is gracious!

I personally believe that many of our pastors who are so-called retiring are really in a position to help train and equip our young pastors and other Christian workers on a solid gospel foundation. Recent Barna research has reflected the following stats:

- In 1992 concerning the age of Protestant clergy, the median age was 44. One in three pastors was under age 40 and 1 in 4 was over 55.

- In 2016 the average age was 54. Only 1 in 7 pastors was under 40, and half are over 55. The percentage of church leaders 65 and older has nearly tripled.

- Today there are more pastors over 65 years of age than there are younger pastors at 40 and below.[14]

Several reasons for this trend were offered:

- People are living longer.

- The increase in "2nd career clergy."

- More pastors are coming to the ministry later in life.[15]

NEW FORMS

Dissatisfied with some of the old wineskin denominational churches, many of the young pastors are trying new forms of worship and service. Unlike their old church-minded predecessors; most are more kingdom-minded. America has a complex society. Our population is probably the most diverse and multicultural of any nation in the world – ethnically, religiously, socially, and economically. The challenges associated with such diversity have demanded a stiff price on pastors and other church workers. Notice a few of these challenges:

- The differing and often conflicting values and belief systems are distorted by atheism, secular humanism and multiculturalism. Many times the challenge is another gospel being introduced. A major task of all pastors, Bible teachers and other Christian workers is to keep the Word of God doctrinally pure – thus insuring that the church or ministry is on a sound foundation. Many true children of God have been engaged even unto death for almost two thousand years faithfully committed to that task.

- A negative attitude toward God's moral law which is plaguing this nation today.

- The process of assimilating people into a progressive cultural mix with the local churches is proving to be a very difficult challenge as is apparent in the fast growing disparities between the young and old, rich and poor, educated and uneducated, married and single, carnal-minded and spiritual-minded, multiculturalism and Christianity.

- The rising tension between authentic Christianity and pseudo-religious Christianity [cultural], conservatives and liberals, legitimacy and illegitimacy, the cultural worldview and Christian worldview.

- Having traveled internationally over the years I believe America is probably the only nation in recent times to yield their founding faith for another namely Multiculturalism. Multiculturalism has rendered that all faiths are equal. The idea seems to be to crowd out Christianity.

- Rising racial and ethnic tensions continue to trouble the nation, in spite of gains made.

Since the presidential election hostilities, mistrust, and apathy have been on the rise along with a "we/ they" attitude. However, God's true leaders are alright because in all generations there are God-fearing,

Spirit-filled saints who hear what the Spirit is saying to His churches. Nations come and go but the Church of the Living God remains and will remain until Christ returns to take her home.

FROM THE CRADLE TO THE GRAVE

God's main deterrent against sin remains blood-washed, Spirit-filled righteous living Christians. However, the home training is the beginning point for the child's successful Christian life. For the Word of God says,

"Train up a child in the way he should go; and when he [or she] is old they will not depart from it" (see Proverbs 22:6).

This is one of the most misinterpreted verses in the Bible. Perhaps it is due to spiritual ignorance, or rational thinking. This passage contains God's promise. Like many of God's promises, it is linked to a command:

The Command: *"Train up a child in the way he [or she] should go!"* It is parental responsibility to "train" or "train up" the child.

The promise: *"When he [or she] is old will not depart from it."* It is God's responsibility to "keep" the child. And He will! Providing we do our part and train them up. [Fulfillment of the promise is conditional to the parents obeying His command to "train up"].

This is totally impossible without the enablement of the Holy Spirit and the Word. Emphasis added.

Most churches do not totally deny the Holy Spirit, the divine power Source – but few totally allow Him to fully lead and guide them.

The Spirit and the Word

By comparison my early automobile experience mentioned earlier was similar to many of our local churches today; that attempt to be authentic without the Holy Spirit and the knowledge of the truth. Their validity individually as well as corporately comes into question, because the essential components for life and proper operation are not there. Other congregations are struggling because of other reasons such as:

- Ignorance of God's full plan and story of redemption.

- Ignorance of God's purposes.

- Little knowledge of His Spirit, His Word and His will.

- A low view of Scripture – the Bible has been neglected in the pulpit and the home.

- In many instances members of the congregation may be *intellectually* aware of the teaching of the Bible, but *fail to act on it* accordingly.

- Many members are *intellectually* aware of Scripture, but lack *faith* in God.

- Some congregations *fail to pursue* God's purposes because, their members understand that God is working to save people and develop them into His disciples, but they *falsely believe* that He has no active part for them in this work.

This type of misunderstanding of God's sovereignty prevails in many churches today; they reach a point where they merely sit back to watch how God decides to use His will. You hear such clichés as "Let the Spirit have His way!" "If God wants us to grow; He'll send the people." These folk fail to pursue God's purposes and are consequently deprived of the power of the Spirit and the Word they could have been enjoying had they been given the knowledge of the truth of their supernatural *[can't do it without the Spirit and the Word]* responsibility to edify the saved and evangelize the lost. In Romans 5:5, we learn that when we were saved God poured His love into our hearts and gave us the Holy Spirit. Thus, He has given us all the enablement *[love* and *power]* that we need for the transition from the natural to the spiritual (see Romans 6:11; 2 Corinthians 5:17).

We desperately need the practical admonition of the apostle Paul: *"Lead a life worthy of the calling to which you have been called"* (Ephesians 4:1). The One who called us sees life much clearer than we do. The Lord has devised a strategy that will actually destroy the roots of all of this human darkness and misery. When the church individually and corporately is faithful to its calling, it becomes the supernatural healing agent in society.

Edifying one another

*"Let no corrupt word proceed out of your mouth, but what is good for necessary **edification,** that it may impart **grace** to the hearers"* (Ephesians 4:29). Emphasis added.

In the Greek the word for *edification* is *"oikodomeo,"* which denotes the act of building (*oikos,* "a home," and *demo,* to build); this is used only figuratively in the New Testament, in the sense of edification, the promotion of **spiritual growth** ("building up"), (see Roman 14:19; 15:2; 1 Corinthians 14:3, 5, 12, 26).[16] Emphasis added.

The Christian's mouth should be instructive, encouraging, uplifting [even when it must be corrective] and suited for that moment. We are called to "build up" one another just as a house is built one brick at a time. We are called to promote spiritual growth and development in other believers. We must help one another simply because God designed the church to work that way.

We flourish under the loving care of each other and we wither away when we try to be a lone ranger. This way we impart grace to the hearers, and because we have been saved by grace, and kept by grace, we should speak with grace – which is the Lord's standard (see Luke 4:22).

The ultimate tools for building up one another are the Spirit and the truth of God's Word working in tandem through each Christian. To tear something down requires no skill at all – we who have received the Holy Spirit and love of God in our hearts (Romans 5:5), must be the builders. Early Christians made the marketplace the focal point of their ministry. According to Ed Silvoso this was natural since they regularly went there to conduct business.

It was also the place for them to witness to unbelievers. However, according to the Scriptures they did more than witness, as we understand the Word today. They performed signs and wonders in the marketplace. He reports that of the twenty-two power encounters recorded in the book of Acts, only one happened in a religious venue, the healing of the lame seated at the Temple Gate called Beautiful (see Acts 3:1-11).[17]

CHAPTER 5 REVIEW: GETTING A HANDLE ON REALITY

1. Discuss the aging of American pastors.
2. Discuss the difference between Church-mindedness and Kingdom-mindedness.
3. Define multiculturalism.
4. Discuss the necessity of keeping the church doctrinally pure.
5. Discuss the command and promise in Proverbs 22:6 in reference to parents and children.

CHAPTER SIX

THE CHURCH WITHIN THE CHURCH

"Again, the kingdom of heaven is like unto a net, that was cast into the sea, and gathered of every kind" (Matthew 13:47).

I will be repeating some statements discussed in an earlier chapter concerning the two kingdoms as represented in the world. They are the kingdom of Heaven represented by the second Adam, Jesus Christ, and the kingdom of the world ruled by the now prince of this world, Satan.

The real Church is the *ekklesia*, the community of people *called out* to walk in intimate relationship with God and His Son through and by the power of the Holy Spirit. In reality, a colony of the kingdom of Heaven is located in the world, but is not of the world. It has been said, "If you want to find the church it is in the world; and if you want to find the world it is in the church." That may be true of the physical church, but definitely untrue of the true Spiritual church universal, the body of Christ.

The true Church

The true church does not take its cue from the world or the culture, but in relationship with God the church *radiates* blessing to the rest of its society and the world. Whole cultures are fed from the real churches' releasing of truth, love, grace, justice, freedom and all the other fruits it yields. The Scriptures reveal what happens when the House of God determines the quality of life for the whole society.

Although that is a determined fact, again I say, "multiculturalism at its core claims that all faiths are equal and is so widely accepted here in America; that if not countered, overtime it could bring this nation to destruction." History has shone that if a culture is going to survive it must not destroy its religious roots which birthed the vision out of which it arose. Therefore the strength and stability of a society are related directly to the strength and stability in the case of America, the biblically-based church.

Prayers of Intercession

I believe America and the West is the depository of Christianity. However, demonic forces are working 24/7 to destroy that foundational truth, by pushing secularism, and the promotion of biblical illiteracy. However, these biblical truths are conserved by Bible-believing churches and ministries. When Solomon built the temple in Jerusalem, God told Him,

"If I shut up the heavens so that there is no rain, or if I command the locust to devour the land, or if I send pestilence among My people, and if My people who are called by My name would humble themselves and pray and seek My face and turn from their wicked ways, then I will her from heaven, and I will forgive their sin and will heal their land. Now My eyes will open and My ears attentive to the prayers offered in this place. For now I have chosen and consecrated this house that My name may be there forever, and My eyes and My heart will be there perpetually" (2 Chronicles 7:13-16).

Jesus told His followers they were the "light of the world." Paul conveyed the same reality message when he wrote, "You were formerly darkness, but now you are light in the Lord; walk as children of Light" (Ephesians 5:8).

In Revelation 5:8, John's visions definitely impact the church and provide a schematic outline of the world's history and events. He saw at the throne of God *"golden bowls full of incense, which are the **prayers of the saints.**"* Emphasis added throughout.

A Holy Priesthood

The Scriptures describe the community of true believers as a holy priesthood. Peter wrote, "Coming to Him as to a living stone which has been rejected by men, but is choice and precious in the sight of God, you also, as living stones, are being built up as a spiritual house for a holy priesthood, to offer up ***spiritual sacrifices*** acceptable to God through Jesus Christ" (1 Peter 2:4-5).

Metaphorically, God is building a spiritual house, putting all true believers in place, integrating each one with others, and each one with the life of Christ (see Ephesians 2:19; Hebrews 3:6). Old Testament priests and New Testament believer priests:

- Priesthood is an elect privilege (see Exodus 2:19; John 15:16).
- Priests are cleansed of sins (see Leviticus 8:6-36; Titus 2:14).
- Priests are clothed for service (see 1 Peter 5:5; Exodus 28:42; Leviticus 8:7; Psalm 132:9, 16).
- Priests are anointed for service (see Leviticus 8:12, 30; 1 John 2:20, 27).
- Priests are prepared for service (see Leviticus 8:33; 9:4, 23; Galatians 1:16; 1 Timothy 3:6).
- Priests are ordained to obedience (see 1 Peter 2:4; Leviticus 10:1).
- Priests are to honor the Word of God (see 1 Peter 2:2; Malachi 2:7).
- Priests are to walk with God (see Malachi 2:6; Galatians 5:16, 25).
- Priests are to impact sinners (Malachi 2:6; Galatians 6:1).
- Priests are to be messengers of God (see Malachi 2:7; Matthew 28:19, 20).

The primary privilege of a priest is access to God.

MYSTERY OF THE KINGDOM

The parable of the "net" presents a view of the mystery of the kingdom. The kingdom is depicted as an admixture which is more the results of the tendency of a movement to gather to itself that which is not really of it. The kingdom of heaven is like a net, which cast into the sea of humanity, gathers of every kind, good and bad; and these remain together in the net until the end of the age (see Matthew 13:49-50).

Thus, in this sphere the church is located during this age. It is a mingled body of true and false, good and bad. While it is defined by formalism, traditionalism, and today's growing biblical illiteracy, doubt, and worldliness – within it Christ sees the children of the true kingdom of God who at the end will "shine forth as the sun." He also sees:

- The redeemed of all ages
- His hidden Israel, yet to be restored
- He sees the Church, His body and Bride

Herein we find the explanation for the utter confusion in some local churches today. Within the membership are the true believers, some unbelievers, the hypocrites, the backsliders, the apostates, and the pseudo-religious Christians. How can we get a handle on such a paradox? How can the church be both riddled with sin *and* salt and light?

How can the church be both a source of disillusionment and a source of illumination at the same time? The answers to these questions are found in the Word of God: What we so popularly call "the church" is actually two churches. So in reality in the kingdom the local churches are a mixture of both:

- In one we find selfish, jealousy, power-seeking, hatred, conflict after conflict, and persecution all in the name of God.
- In the other church we find those who always work to save others, heal human hurts, deliver people from their guilt, shame, fear, spiritual and biblical ignorance, and breakdown walls of prejudice of any kind.

One is a pseudo-religious Satan substitute masquerading as Church which mirrors (the "works of the flesh" as listed in Galatians 5:17-21) and the other is the true Church founded by Jesus Christ, mirroring His character through acts of love, other graces, and truth (see the "Fruit of the Spirit" in Galatians 5:22-23).

For some unknown reason we are continually surprised when we are confronted by the counterfeit church. Sometimes this confrontation causes some authentic church folk to begin to doubt their salvation and the reality of God. We are not to be surprised or disillusioned when we come up against counterfeit Christianity. Jesus Himself predicted such encounters.

In Matthew 13, Jesus used a series of parables to describe conditions in the world during the time between His first and second coming. We now live in that age in between. One of His parables is called the parable of the wheat and the tares. In this story, Jesus Himself says, as the Son of Man, He plants wheat in the field of the world. The wheat represents Christians, whom He calls "the sons of the kingdom."

After the wheat is planted, the devil comes along and plants tares [his weeds] which looks like wheat but produces no grain [fruit]. The wheat and the tares grow up together, and for a period of time they are completely indistinguishable from each other.

Soon workers notice the weeds growing among the wheat and come asking if they should dig them up – but the Lord answers: NO! Uprooting the tares would destroy the wheat along with the weeds. Instead, *"let both grow together until the harvest"* (Matthew 13:30).

The harvest Jesus is speaking of will come at the end of the age when He sends His angels [not people] into the field [world] to separate the weeds from the wheat. The weeds to be burned in the judgment and the wheat will be gathered into His Father's barns. The wheat, the true Christians, the sons of the kingdom are those who have experienced the new birth (see John 3:3). Peter describes the genuine Christians as being "born anew, not of perishable seed but of imperishable, through the living and abiding Word of God" (I Peter 1:23).

Of course the sons of the evil one are the false Christians, never born again by the power of the Holy Spirit through faith in the Word of God, but say they are Christians because they have:

- Performance of outward rituals
- Joined a local church
- Outward covering of religiosity

In God's sight they are the devil's children. To other people, even to themselves I am sad to say, they are indistinguishable from the true Christians. If we continue to ignore the biblical picture [the wheat and the tares] of the church as so many Christian Communities are doing by viewing these two distinct churches *as one and the same,* then we are doomed to a kind of "mixed seed" that will continue to baffle and confuse people. The result of this confusion has been *cold* love in the church and growing increasingly colder along with the absence of the Spirit. Several causes for conflict seem to be reoccurring in many local churches:

- through biblical and spiritual illiteracy
- choosing to assimilate with the non-Christian world
- failure to be faithful
- failure to obey the Lord's commands

Many local churches have wandered so far off their true purpose that for a couple of generations now the members have been asking, "Who are we? And why are we here?"

CHOOSE LIFE "IN CHRIST" [TRUE CHRISTIANITY]

As many may think, the division between true church and counterfeit church does not lie along denominational lines. Authentic Christianity is not a matter of organizations or groups. Some may say the real Christian or counterfeit will eventually manifest. Certainly it is not that simple. Of course, it is true, biblically counterfeit Christians can only manifest counterfeit Christianity. However, through willful disobedience or biblical ignorance, true Christians are able to manifest both true and false Christianity – but not at the same time. When they do so, they cause much more confusion and harm for the unregenerate around them – and bringing dishonor to their Lord and Savior.

Since Pentecost, believers are received into the true Church, through regeneration, that is being "born of the Spirit from above." Again, like the net there are many different people in the church, but only three categories, the natural, the spiritual, and the carnal each with their own distinct perspective:

Natural man – Greek *psuchikos,* "of the five senses" or "natural" the Adam man:

- The unregenerate person in spirit, soul, and body are centered on self, prone to sin, and opposed to God – need the "new birth" (John 3:3, 5). The Scripture is completely hidden from this person.
- His or her wisdom descends not from above, but is earthly, sensual, devilish (James 3:15).
- These are those who separate themselves, sensual, having not the Spirit (Jude 19).

Spiritual man – Greek *pneumatikos,* "the regenerate person is saved" (John 3:3, 5):

- His or her wisdom descends from above (James 33:15).
- The regenerated person is "not walking after the flesh, but after the Spirit" (Romans 8:4).
- He or he is Spirit-filled and walking in Spirit and truth in full communion with God (Ephesians 5:18-20).

Carnal man – Greek *sarkikos,* the Christian walking "after the flesh," is able to comprehend only the simplest "truths" of Scripture:

- Remains a "babe in Christ" (see 1 Corinthian 3:1-2).
- This person still has envy, strife, divisions and walks as the unregenerate (see v. 6).

To be carnally minded is death, but to be spiritually minded is life and peace. Because the carnal mind is enmity against God; for it is not subject to the law of God, nor indeed can be. So then, those who are in the flesh cannot please God (study carefully Romans 8:6-8).

Free from indwelling sin

"But you are not in the flesh but in the Spirit, *if indeed* the Spirit of God *dwells* in you. Now if anyone does not have the Spirit of Christ, he is not His. And if Christ is in you, the body is dead because of sin, but the Spirit of Him who raised Jesus from the dead will also give life to your mortal bodies through His Spirit who *dwells in you"*(vv. 9-11). Emphasis added throughout.

Led by the Holy Spirit

The Bible does not teach that believers are led through subjective, mental impressions or some prompting to give direction in making the decisions of life. For the true Christian believers are led by the Spirit of God objectively:

- Sometimes He orchestrates through circumstances (see Acts 16:7).
- In most cases He divinely reveals the meaning of Scripture to make it understandable to our finite minds (see Ephesians 1:17-20).
- The inner voice of the Holy Spirit (see 1 Samuel :10).

Christ's eternal kingdom

A key theme of the Book of Ephesians is the mystery of the church, which is,

"That the Gentiles should be fellow heirs, of the same body, and partakers of His promise in Christ through the gospel" (Ephesians 3:6).

All believers in Jesus Christ, the Messiah, are equal before the Lord as His children and as citizens of His eternal kingdom, a magnificent truth that only believers of this present age possess. Another truth emphasized by Paul is that the church is Christ's present spiritual, earthly body; also a distinct and former mystery about God's people. The metaphor depicts:

- The church, not as an organization, but as a living organism composed of mutually related and interdependent parts.
- Christ is the Head of the Church, which is His body and the Holy Spirit is the life blood.
- The body functions through the faithful use of its members' various spiritual gifts, sovereignty, all uniquely bestowed by the Holy Spirit on each believer – we will further explore the Holy Spirit and His gifts and ministries in chapters 10-11;

also (carefully study Ephesians 4:11-13; 1 Corinthians 12:1-12; Romans 12:6-9).

The local church

One of the major problems many local churches face today is that the people have so emphasized a personal relationship with the Lord that they have *lost* their sense of corporate identity. More and more Christians are beginning to think they stand alone before God and that they are not accountable to anyone else, including the church.

Though Christians do have access to God through Christ as their one Mediator; God created the church as His redemptive agent in the world. He has a purpose for the church; therefore, God places every member in a church to accomplish His redemptive purposes *through* that church. A church is a body:

- It is the body of Christ (1 Corinthians 12:27).
- Jesus Christ is present as the Head of the church through His Devine Emissary, the Holy Spirit (Ephesians 4:15).
- Every member is placed in the body as it pleases God, the Holy Spirit (I Corinthians 12:18).
- The Holy Spirit manifest Himself to all for the common good (I Corinthians 12:7).
- The whole body is fitted together by the Father and by the Holy Spirit who enables and equips each member to function where the Father has placed them in the body.
- The body then functions to build itself up into the Head, until every member comes to the measure of the stature of the fullness of Christ (see Ephesians 4:13).

God made each member mutually interdependent; and therefore we need each other. What one member lacks, others in the body can supply. By design what God is doing in and through the body is essential to our knowing how to respond to Him. Where we see God working in the body, we are to adjust and put our life there corporately. God chose to complete His work in each member. That was Paul's intent when he said,

"Him we preach, warning every man and teaching every man in all wisdom, that we may present every man perfect in Christ Jesus" (Colossians 1:28).

Paul was constantly admonishing the believers to become faithfully involved with his life and ministry. The effectiveness of Paul's ministry rested on them (carefully study Colossians 4:3; 2 Thessalonians 3:1, 2; Ephesians 6:19).

I have known some people who have accepted the Lord through individuals sincerely witnessing, separate from the church, however, they do not have a pastor or church to take them or even to refer them to. Apart from the body, you cannot know God's will for your relationship to the body of Christ. Without the Head the left hand cannot communicate to the right hand to help it lift a box, because the word to do so must come from the Head. So the need is communicated to the Head, who in turn communicates it to the right hand.

All the members of the body belong to each other, and they need each other! Sometimes God speaks through other believers and the church to help you know what His will and assignment is; that you are to carry out in the ministry of the kingdom.

A New Nature

"Little children, let no man deceive you!" Pseudo-religious Christianity was trying to convince true believers that a person could be "saved" and still practice sin. This is widely held in many local churches across this land today. The apostle John in no way implies that Christians do not sin – but he does deny that Christians can *live in sin.* A person who can enjoy deliberate sin and does not *feel convicted* or *experience God's chastening* had better examine himself or herself to see whether or not he or she is really born of God from above. Little emphasized in churches today is the fact that believers do not practice sin because he or she has *a new nature within,* and that new nature *cannot* sin. John calls this new nature God's *"seed."*

When a person receives Christ as Savior tremendous *spiritual* changes take place within them. He or she is given a new standing before God, being accepted as righteous in God's sight. This new standing is called **"justification."** It never changes and is never lost. The new Christian is also given a new position; he or she is "set apart" for God's own purposes to live for His glory. This new position is called **"sanctification,"** and it has a way of changing because it is not stagnant. Some days we are closer to the Lord than others and more readily obey Him. Of the spiritual changes in the new believer the most dramatic change is called **"regeneration."** He or she is **"born again"** from above, into the family of God ["re" means "again," and "generation" means "birth" to life]. In summary:

- Justification means a new *standing [born again]* before God.
- Sanctification means being *set apart* to God for His glory.
- Regeneration means a new *nature* – God's nature (see 2 Peter 1:4).

The only way to enter the family of God is by repentance, trusting Christ, and experiencing the new birth. The Scripture says,

"Whosoever believes that Jesus is the Christ is born of God" (1 John 5:1).

Remember, physical life produces physical life – and spiritual life produces spiritual life.

"That which is born of the flesh is flesh; and that which is born of the Spirit is spirit" (John 3:6).

Our new Parents

Christians have been born again, "not of corruptible seed, but of incorruptible, by the Word of God, who lives and abides forever" (see I Peter 1:23). The Christian now has new [*spiritual*] parents, **the Word of God** and **the Spirit of God.**

The Spirit of God uses the Word of God to convict of sin and to reveal the Savior.

We are saved by faith: *"For by grace you have been saved through faith, and that not of yourselves; it is the gift of God"* (Ephesians 2:8, 9).

So then faith comes by hearing: *and hearing by the Word of God"* (Romans 10:17).

Just like physical children inherit the nature of their parents, so God's spiritual children receives His nature in regeneration. Thus, a Christian has an old nature from his or her physical birth and a new nature from his or her spiritual birth. The old nature produces sin – but the new nature leads one into holy living. A Christian is responsible to live according to his or her new nature – not the old nature.

A Christian's responsibility is to live according to her or his new nature, not the old nature.

A Christian who feeds their new nature from the Spirit and the Word of God will have power to live a godly life. Paul tells us to,

"Put on the Lord Jesus Christ, and make no provision for the flesh, to fulfill the lusts thereof" (Romans 13:14).

This verse summarizes *sanctification,* the continuing spiritual process in which those who haven been saved by faith are *transformed* into the likeness of Christ. Just as we stand before the mirror frequently washing our face and hands, as believers:

- We must spiritually look into the mirror of God's Word daily, examine ourselves, and adjust our lives accordingly (James 1:22-25).

- We must confess our sins and claim God's forgiveness (I John 1:9).

Otherwise the "inner man" [new nature] becomes unclean and this uncleanness will make you "spiritually sick, weak and open to:

- **Backsliding** – which is a gradual move away from a close walk with Christ which if not countered will lead to a life filled with worldliness and unconfessed sins?

- **Spiritual deficiency** – we lose our appetite for spiritual things, again if not countered we become listless and finally yield to the sin (see James 1:14).

The only way to counter this malady is to confess and forsake our sin and turn to Christ for cleansing and healing. "Exercise yourself .....

unto godliness" (1 Timothy 4:7). A person who eats but does not exercise will become flabby and out of shape – a person who exercises without eating will kill him or herself. There must be a proper balance. "Spiritual exercise," for a believer includes:

- Sharing Christ with others
- Doing good works in Christ's name
- Helping to build up other believers
- Exercise your spiritual gift for the good and build up of the church (1 Corinthians 12:1-11).

Good Stewards

The Apostle Peter exhorts, *"As each one has received a gift, minister it to one another, as good stewards of the manifold grace of God"* (I Peter 4:10).

A spiritual gift is a graciously given supernatural ability granted to every true believer by which the Holy Spirit ministers to the body of Christ. Again, a spiritual gift cannot be earned, pursued or worked out. It is a freely-given gift merely received through the grace of God from the Holy Spirit as He sees fit for you *to manage* for the church to the glory of God (see 1 Corinthians 12:4, 18).

Today many local churches are confusing *natural talents, skills, and abilities* such as are possessed by believers and unbelievers alike. Spiritual gifts are *supernaturally* given by the Holy Spirit *sovereignly* as He wills to all true believers (carefully study vv. 7, 11). Emphasis is added throughout.

These gifts are not to be used for the exaltation of the person with the gift or gifts, but to enable each believer to spiritually edify [build up] each other effectively and thus honor the Lord in loving concern for the benefit of others in the church (review chapters 11 and 12 of this book for a more through explanation on the Holy Spirit and His spiritual gifts and ministry). Satan has used many of his counterfeit Christians to confuse and abuse authentic Christianity around the world – by mocking or parroting true spiritual giftedness.

CHAPTER 6 REVIEW: THE CHURCH WITHIN THE CHURCH

1. Explain the Church as a colony of the kingdom of heaven on earth.
2. Discuss Jesus' parable of the "net."
3. The Scripture is completely hidden from the unregenerate.
4. Discuss the three categories of people on the earth according to the apostle Paul.
5. The Christian believers are led by the Spirit of God objectively. Sometimes He leads through the orchestration of circumstances. In most cases He leads through the Scriptures.

CHAPTER SEVEN

WHY ARE WE HERE?

"All Scripture is given by inspiration of God, and is profitable for doctrine, for reproof, for correction, for instruction in righteousness, that the man of God may be complete, thoroughly equipped for every good work" (2 Timothy 3:16-17).

It has been said, "Forget the crisis of the past; and you will surely repeat it." While we are not Israel, we can learn much about God and His dealing with His children through the Old Testament. Also we learn much about the old raw Adam nature that shows up in many people within the local churches today.

The tendency in the O.T. seems to be the people would fall into sin trying to live without God, only to fall, after total failure upon His mercy [not giving them what they deserved] but through grace [which they did not deserve] gave them another chance. I found as I read through the Minor Prophets and Judges a reciprocal trend of this.

Today God is merciful, and people love grace, but abuses it having no desire to neither repent nor live under the Lord. Like ancient Israel, America is in crisis. From coast to coast no matter which side of the political aisle you sit; it is apparent that things are spiraling downward at a catastrophic speed.

The United States of America is very quickly becoming the divided states of America as signs of disunity and conflict amplifies just how wide-spread Satan's sinful contamination really is. Carefully note a few of his foot prints below:

- Sunday is made a workday like the other six days
- Sunday brunch with drinks at ten oclock
- Legal justice is acceptable over Moral justice
- The marriage and the family breakdown
- Intergenerational communications crisis
- The abiding racial divide
- The secularization of culture and society
- Rise of earthly [social] wisdom
- Continuing moral decay
- The redefining of all foundational institutions
- The media continues to dumb down decency
- An educational system that imparts information without ethics while shouting "freedom."
- No absolutes
- Striving to ban God, Christ, Christianity, and the things of God from the public square.
- Blurring of gender from God's distinct differences of gender to [sameness].
- The demise of the Judeo-Christian ethic and worldview.
- Legality over morality.
- The constant threat of terrorism.
- The vanishing future of our grandchildren and great-grandchildren.

CAN THESE BONES LIVE?

History shows many nations have reached the situation of almost hopelessness that we seem to be experiencing today in America. The Holy Spirit gives us a rear view look into Israel's past wherein everything had become hopeless and near death; during their exile in Babylon (see 2 Kings 24:10-16).

The people had been lulled into despair and apathy. They were at a point where they would roll over and forget any kind of hope they had previously sought. To them there was no way out of the darkness that surrounded them. God sent a vision of a dry valley filled with dry bones to Ezekiel. We can examine it in Ezekiel chapter 37:

The hand of the Lord was upon me, and He brought me out by the Spirit of the Lord and set me down in the middle of the valley; and it was full of bones. He caused me to pass among them round about, and behold, there were very many on the surface of the valley; and lo, they were very dry (vv. 1-2).

In order for the bones to be dry indicates that they had been there for a long time. This raises two questions, why were they there so long? And what did they represent? We get the answer in v.11. Then He said to me,

"Son of man, these bones is the whole house of Israel; behold, they say, "Our bones are dried up and our hope has perished. We are completely cut off."

Many local churches today, like these exiles have maintained a form of religion, but have lost their relationship with God through rebellion and they are "cut off." However, it was God's desire to return them to Himself as we read in (verse 23). The nation had been "cut off" because they decided to replace the one true God with other gods, or to bring other gods alongside Him; certainly this had a diminishing affect on their lives.

Multiculturalism is flourishing in this country – but so are [the gods of the multi-cultures].

The nation's sin had worked itself out into their society, as they lived in exile. The situation was so bad for the exiles that when God asked the prophet Ezekiel if the bones could live – the prophet's answer was in essence reserved like his people, "I don't know" (v. 3).

They had found themselves in a situation with no solution. Only God knew if this situation could get turned around. Only God knew if the valley of dry bones could live again. And they had a spiritual disconnect. A few months back, we had a similar situation in our State wherein in big money was actually holding the state hostage in my estimation, by threatening to hold back key national sports events from our cities unless the State's General Assembly repealed HB-2, known also as the bathroom bill; wherein the individual would be allowed to use the public restrooms and locker room facilities of his or her gender orientation or choice.

A check of secular humanism's agenda[18] reflects that the repeal would work well with their agenda goals. The idea of pedophiles taking advantage of children and the safety of all people in general from the solicitation and temptation of sinful activities are not at issue with them. Greed is the decisive factor here as in many other situations that the culture prioritize above the public's safety. This outlook is in keeping with the humanistic view "get all you can" and "enjoy all you get to the fullest for tomorrow you die."

A case in point, several months ago, Fox News reported that a 14 year old girl was raped in her own home by two illegal immigrants; the incident was not carried by any other major news outlet. In fact what was carried by them and heard around the world was the fact that many people took sides with the culprits because they were called illegal immigrants which discriminates against all others of illegal status. Come on somebody, what about the 14 year old girl and her family – will they be able to survive this trauma?

PREPARED FOR GLORY

What we must do now is get our eyes off the darkness around us, a darkness which is deepening on the world – and live in personal victory to the utmost in the light that God has given us. If we could look from the throne of God down upon the world, we would see the Holy Spirit moving here and there, "pouring out" wherever He can get an outlet.

As the eyes of our heart are illuminated, we shall not be deceived by what we see on the surface of civilization today and imagine "the world is getting better." Neither should you be surprised to find that the religious "Christianity" of today *will* stone the prophets, and crucify Christ afresh as did the Jews so long ago. Pseudo-religious Christianity will always turn upon the *true,* but in the light of the Ascended Lord you can survive the stones.

When Stephen was dying he saw Jesus standing to receive him. Notice, the Lord who was seated rose to receive the spirit of His *faithful witness.*

It is worth being stoned to see Jesus, our Lord standing to receive you!

BLESSINGS OF PENTECOST

We are going to have the stones which actually were a blessing of Pentecost along with the blessing of the Holy Spirit in the winning of many souls. Are you prepared for them?

- We want the blessing of winning souls, but
- We chose the honor of the stones

We sort of take for granted those who are martyred in the Middle East or China today, but be warned, God has His martyrs right here in the United States who are being stoned but in the civilized manner today. Stand in the Spirit and truth of God's Word and the stones will fly. Don't be afraid of the persecution, scoffing, opposition or the rejection. God allows these stones of rejection by the prince of this world to drive His children out of the earthly realm to live in glory with Him.

Grounded on the Rock

Now that we see the glory side – it is appropriate for us to review the foundation and make sure that we are grounded on the rock of Calvary; which is found in (Romans 6:3):

"Do you not know that as many of us as were baptized into Christ Jesus were baptized into His death?"

You can not be "raised from the dead" unless you have died. Therefore, you must fully understand that it is impossible to share in Christ's resurrection unless you have also shared in the fellowship of His death. The believer's foundation is in His death – this is where you must be rooted and planted, so that no storm can ever pull you out. It has been said that the oak tree lengthens its roots in storms. Like the oak tree, God puts us through many storms; and His putting our roots to the tests strengthens them. Paul used the word "baptized" in this verse in a metaphorical sense as we might say someone was immersed in his work, or as we would say to a soldier in Vietnam after he had survived His first firefight against the enemy, "that he was baptized under fire."

Having these explanations, do you know what it means for the Holy Spirit to take you and put you into the death of Christ – not in an outward and visible way, but in the real likeness of His death? Paul makes this "likeness" clear in (verse 5):

"If we have been united together in the likeness of His death, certainly we also shall be in the likeness of His resurrection."

Standing in Christ

In an earlier section I stated that the unsaved person can only sin because that is his or her nature to do so. However, the saved can sin and live holy, but not at the same time. In opening his letter to the Corinthian Church, Paul reminded them of the wonderful blessings they had in Christ:

- They are sanctified in Christ Jesus, and called to be saints (1:2).
- Then he reproves them for their sin, because they were living beneath their privileges as Christians (see 1 Corinthians 1:1).
- They were not walking in a manner worthy of their *calling in Christ* (see Ephesians 4:1).
- They were waiting for Christ to return, but they were not living like saints (see 1 John 2:28).

The church at Corinth mirrored many of our local churches today, by the grace of God they were wonderfully blessed with spiritual gifts; especially the sign gifts (see chapters 12-14). Yet with all their gifts and knowledge, they lacked love (see 13:1-3). It is imperative that our churches realize that "gifts are given" by the Holy Spirit, but the "fruit of the Spirit are developed in our new nature, by the Spirit. Paul points out to this church [and us] that by ignoring the graces [fruit] they were depriving themselves of spiritual power.

According to 1 Corinthians 1:9, "the strength of His might" is the very strength that lifted Christ from the dead and set Him on the right hand of the Father – can enter into your spirit and lift it to the place of victory. Give Him praise and glory!

CHAPTER 7 REVIEW: WHY ARE WE HERE?

1. Discuss Satan's widespread contamination in the church today.
2. Discuss conditions of the children of Israel when God gave Ezekiel the vision of the valley of dry bones.
3. The nation of Israel had been "cut-off" because they decided to replace the One true God with other gods or at least place Him alongside them.
4. Discuss being in the likeness of Christ in His resurrection.
5. You cannot be raised from the dead unless you have died.

SECTION III

BECAUSE WE ARE NOT THERE

CHAPTER EIGHT

BECAUSE WE ARE NOT THERE

There is a way that seems right to man, but the end thereof are the ways of death (Proverbs 14:12).

Hundreds of churches and ministries are closing their doors permanently each year. It's ironic in a day when more Christian resources are available to the churches than ever could be read or applied in a lifetime. The internet has replaced the "How To" books on the unchurched and how to win them. If you have a question this present generation would tell you to "just goggle it!"

Yet many churches struggle and fail as they make attempts to be transformers in their local areas of influence both individually and corporately. One pastor told me that he had not baptized anyone in the last couple of years. Research reveals 2.5 million people die each year in the United States. Only God knows where each person will spend eternity. The same report estimates that over 70% of these people will go into eternity without Christ. Many of these people were denied the opportunity to be taught the graces and be discipled in their personal journey with the knowledge of our Lord and Savior, Jesus Christ.

This condition must be taken very seriously, lay aside your prevailing understandings of evangelism and simply follow the Great Commission as your guide. As New Testament believer-priests or ministers of reconciliation, we should *all* simply disciple people everywhere we go. The salvation of the individual is God's part in the process – our part in the process is to devote significant time and commitment to making disciples of whoever wants to take the journey with us.

Because something has been practiced for a thousand years does not mean it is right; and because it has not been practiced for a thousand years does not mean it's wrong.

This journey is about Jesus, and we get to share the gospel [the saving message of Jesus] along the way. We must consider evangelism within the framework of discipleship. That's where it belongs in the Bible. The only solution to bringing down the number of people dying without Christ is to take seriously our responsibilities individually and corporately to get them saved; otherwise if we allow discipleship to drop off the church's mission, we simply become what Jude called, "clouds without water" and the church within one generation can actually forget its own mandate and die:

MAKING DISCIPLES

Many churches have moved from under the umbrella of the New Testament. Therefore they are too busy doing their own thing to concern themselves with the Scriptural mandates of Christ in reference to love [*agape*] and the Gospel [*evangel*], He commanded that:

"You shall love the Lord your God with all your heart, with all your soul, and with all your mind. This is the first and Great Commandment. And the second is like it: You shall love your neighbor as yourself, on these two commandments hang all the Law and the prophets" (Matthew 22:37-40).

Jesus summed up all moral responsibilities in the word "love," expressed in the twofold directions of God and neighbor. I will list a few among many major hindrances to witnessing and making disciples in the local churches:

1. Heading the list of hindrances is *cold love* for Christ and people. Cold love manifests itself in "selfishness and pride." This type of love is not biblical.

2. We add to the list is a lack of "agape" love; there will be little or *no passion* for souls especially for those who are already in the church. The non-spiritual condition of such persons will never get a handle on, "who is my neighbor?" In the absence of *observable* love, teaching, and application will result in biblical truths not being passed on to the next generation (see Deuteronomy 6:4-5). Jesus gave, the Great Commission to the whole body of Christ!

3. Another hindrance among many to discipleship of all of God's people is the assigning of ministry and leadership to the role of men. Many problems are directly related to this unbiblical arrangement of ordination; which puts over half of the church out of commission. The Bible ascribes all of us to a royal priesthood, all of us to be filled with the Holy Spirit, all of are given spiritual gifts, and all of us are to witness and go make disciples.

4. As I mentioned in an earlier section; there is a glaring gap in many local churches between justification (born again) and sanctification (spiritual maturity through the Spirit and the Word, in discipleship). It is imperative that the whole body be released to the Spirit in order to fulfill God's purposes.

5. My wife and I have been in ministry partnership for many years. Both of us experienced a clear call to serve God with a lifetime commitment. It was never about one of us being in ministry supported by the other. We cut hindrances and represent God much more successfully together than we ever could apart.

"Go make disciples of all nations, baptizing them in the name of the Father, and the Son, and the Holy Spirit and teaching them to obey everything that I have commanded ...."(Matthew 28:19, 20).

We've got to breakdown down the old stronghold, that discipling is limited to Christians within the context of the church building, and performed by a faithful few. The Great Commission tells us that every one of us is to engage in the role of discipling the nations. Everyone who comes into our area of influence – anywhere!

If it is made clear with every believer that this is the way and then take the biblical mandate seriously, we would have a great number of people growing spiritually and becoming more and more like Jesus and fully under His Lordship. We so easily forget that the sole purpose of the church is to draw people into Christ. C. S. Lewis rightly exhorts us:

It is easy to think that the church has a lot of different objects – education, buildings, missions, holding services ….. [But] the Church exists for nothing else but to draw men into Christ, to make them into little Christs. If they are not doing that all the cathedrals, clergy, missions, sermons, even the Bible itself, are simply a waste of time. God became man for no other purpose. It is even doubtful, you know, whether the whole universe was created for any other purpose. It says in the Bible that the whole universe was made for Christ and that everything is to be gathered together in Him.[19]

If Lewis is correct the whole universe was made for Christ and everything is to be gathered together in Him, therefore the Great Commission is not only about evangelism. That is, simply telling people about Jesus; but it is also about:

- Bringing people closer to Jesus; so they can learn His way.
- Teaching them to obey all that He commanded.
- Loving people and introducing them to the grace and the wonder of God in Christ.
- Helping them to apply God's Word, and the call to action those values therein.
- Helping them to see the beauty of Jesus Christ and His kingdom.

To be like Christ

"But you shall receive power when the Holy Spirit has come upon you; and you shall be witnesses to Me in Jerusalem, and in all Judea, and Samaria, and to the end of the earth" (Acts 1:8).

To be an effective Christian for the Lord, we must know why we are here. "Why are we here?" We are here, [Christlike believers], to reflect Him in the world, and bring lost souls to Christ through word and deed in these Last Days of the church age. I believe we are very near the time when King Jesus will return for His Church. Ask yourself the question, "If I don't take up the cause, who will?"

The Lord is seeking faithful people who:
- Have a living personal relationship with Christ.
- Know that in all things be led and guided by the Spirit and the Word working in tandem.
- Look for faithful people to whom he or she can commit the truth who in turn will pass it on to other faithful people.
- Realize that they must view themselves as Christ's representatives through whom He will link two generations.

As in the Days of Noah [when good people do nothing]

When we look at the world today, it is obvious that we are living in the Last Days. Days with similar conditions of the people as Jesus warned would happen as Satan attacks Christians in our time. Let's look at the current conditions in America which are similar to the conditions in the days of Noah and Lot respectively (see Luke 17:26-30):

*"And as it was in the days of Noah, so it will be also in the days of the Son of man: They ate, they drank, they married wives, they were given in marriage, until the day Noah entered the ark, **"and the flood came and destroyed them all."** Likewise, as it was also in the days of Lot: They ate, they drank, they bought, they sold, they planted, they built, but on the day that Lot went out of Sodom it rained fire and brimstone from heaven **"and destroyed them all."** Even so will it be in the day when the Son of Man is revealed.* Emphasis added throughout.

The day of the Son of Man will be a time of judgment, as were the days of Noah (v. 27) and Lot (17:32). Lot's wife represents those who are attached to earthly things, those whose hearts are still in the world. Like Lot's wife such people will be destroyed (see Genesis 19:29). As the event of which Jesus spoke rapidly approaches – we should passionately carry out our individual and corporate responsibilities in the Father's plan of redemption now that we are empowered with the truth and gifted by the Holy Spirit with great faith, humility and opportunity. As we take a closer look, imagine a pie sliced into three sections with each section representing one of three categories of people on the earth during Noah's day. When the Son of man comes in the air to "rapture" His Church, the people of the world are going to be in the same configuration as those of Noah's day and Lot's day.

Of the three groups, Jesus **did not** address the many **gross sins** that were taking place in the days of Noah and Lot. Not one thing that He does mention is within itself a sin. Likewise, He does not say anything about the many **gross sins** taking place in our day. He only lists the **everyday normal affairs of life:** eating, marrying, buying, selling, planting, and building.

The Old Testament Scriptures state that in the days of Noah and Lot *lawlessness, permissiveness,* and *rebellion* were running rampart. This is normally given as the reason why God had to *destroy them all* in both societies. Similarly, we know and witness a lot of these same evils existing in our society today and they are growing worse.

Read the newspaper in any city or town or listen to any newscast. Yet when comparing our day to those of Noah and Lot, Jesus makes no comment about this fact. Instead His comparison is with the normal *everyday activities* of buying, selling, eating, drinking, marrying, planting and building. I'm sure that you like myself want to understand thoroughly what Jesus meant by His comments. *Why would He warn us about the normal, everyday affairs of life?*

The answer is more important than we may realize. It reveals the very high stakes of the spiritual warfare now taking place all across our nation. If you are wondering about the rapid deterioration of moral values in our society, notice – *Looking into the future, Jesus could see that deterioration, so He warned us of the **cause** ahead of time. The importance of that warning is further emphasized by the fact that God recorded it in His Word!*

In His love – He has warned us!

No doubt many of these normal people are church members. However, Christ condemns them because they put all the ***normal*** *everyday affairs above* a personal relationship with Him. Therefore, just as the people of Noah's day rejected the Word preached by Noah (see Luke 17:26-30) – *"the flood came and destroyed them all."* Noah and his family were saved from the destruction because they were safe where the LORD had put them [in the ark]. Today, unless God places you safe from destruction *"in Christ,"* like those good normal people of Noah's day and Lot's day, you to will be lost. And the situation reads the same for today's good and normal people; who are rejecting Christ and ignoring the gospel message, engulfed in their normal everyday affairs. Christ will come in the air to "rapture" or "catch away speedily" His church as He promised meaning:

- There will be no warning (5:1-10)
- To seize by force, for Satan will try to hinder our rapture to heaven.
- To claim for Himself
- To move to a new place
- To rescue from danger, for the church will not go through the Tribulation (1:10; 5:9).

God gave us this prophetic warning in these Last Days, because He recognized the dangers associated with *over-commitment to these seemingly harmless everyday affairs of life* – the buying, selling, building etc. Remember it is not our involvement in these things that make them sinful; but our sin is over commitment to the self-serving affairs of everyday life, which gradually diminishes our commitment to God and living a righteousness life in accordance with His standards. Undoubtedly, that was the problem in the days of Noah and Lot; and today it is quite evident that we know the cause of the degradation running so rampart in America today – and why we are here? We are here because of misplaced priorities!

Serving God was not the people's first priority. So Jesus is warning us that this same temptation would also be predominant in our day.

God looked down through the corridors of time and prophesied through Jesus how our lives would be dominated by our everyday affairs of life. He knew this was one of the reasons why people were led astray in the days of Noah and Lot.

As I stated earlier they would not listen to Noah nor would they recognize the signs of the times. I am not saying it is wrong to be blessed of God with material things. My wife and I have been blessed through the years. We are to desire God's righteous rule over *all* the earth. God will not be second to anything or to anyone! Study and apply Matthew 6:33:

> *"But seek first the kingdom*
> *of God and His righteousness,*
> *and all these things*
> *shall be added to you."*

UNTIL HE COMES

We *are looking for* Christ to come at any moment. The world is not looking for Him at all; but for the world, the Scripture warns, His coming will be sudden and unexpected, like a thief in the night, but again, not so for believers. Unbelievers are in the dark:

- Their understanding is darkened (Ephesians 4:18; 3:8).
- They love the darkness (John 3:19-21; Ephesians 5:11).
- They are controlled by the powers of darkness (Ephesians 6:12).
- The unbelievers are headed for eternal darkness (Matthew 8:12)

The Christian on the other hand is associated with the light:

- For God is light, and Christ is the Light of the world (John 8:12).
- The Christian is a child of light (Ephesians 5:8-14).
- The change from darkness to light was wrought for the child of God (see 2 Corinthians 4:1-6; Colossians 1:13; 1 Peter 2:9).

Since Christians are of the light and belong to the day, they should live in the light and be ready for Christ's return.

Now or never

Church leadership at every level must come to the realization that discipleship is a *way of life*, not just a suggestion or optional extra for the faithful few:

- It creates an appalling condition in our local churches when we think that we can somehow manage to build churches without spiritual and biblical discipleship. Such thinking is actually a disservice to the authentic Christian Faith.

- As the day of the "rapture" approaches it is imperative that the local churches get back on track by reinstituting evangelism and discipleship in building up the body of Christ. Church leaders are aware of the problems, but many are bound by fear for whatever reasons, customs and traditions of men, and therefore, they refuse to make necessary adjustments. In the military and major industry, when a major problem occurs the immediate response of the leadership is to order a ceasing of operations in that particular area, a "stand down," a time to take stock of methodology, beliefs, policies and practices then make the necessary adjustments and changes before resuming operations. For example: the church should consider converting to small group ministries rather than the old "faithful few" in traditional prayer meetings and Bible studies. Small groups require the whole congregation's involvement. The older traditional methods are not adequate and actually they openly reject or hinder proper implementation of New Testament principles, spiritual gifts and practices for every member ministry involvement.

Know yourself

"Examine yourselves as to whether you are in **the faith***. Test yourselves. Do you not know yourselves that Jesus Christ is in you? Unless indeed you are disqualified. But I trust that you will know that we are not disqualified"* (2 Corinthians 13:5, 6). Emphasis added throughout.

Paul's question is very timely today and should be asked of all who profess to be born again Christians. He asked the Corinthians, ***"Do you not know yourselves?"*** May I ask, ***"Do I not know myself?"*** May I ask you, ***"Do you know yourself?"*** Do you know in your heart *for sure* whether you are genuinely saved or not? If not then according to the Word of God – you are not saved. If we are born again, we *know* we are born again; there is no doubt – that is settled!

Just as surely as you know without a doubt that you are breathing and that your heart is beating – you know whether or not you are a child of God. Paul told Timothy, "......... I know whom I have believed, and am persuaded that He is able to keep that which I have committed unto Him against that day" (II Timothy 1:12). Our assurance is unquestionable and "forever settled in heaven" (see Psalm 119:89). Study carefully the following Scriptures:

*"We **know** that we have passed from death to Life, because we love the brethren. He who does not love his brother abides in death"* (I John 3:14).

*"And by this we **know** that we are of the truth, and shall assure our hearts before Him. 'For if our heart condemns us, God is greater than our heart, and knows all things. Beloved, if our heart does not condemn us, we have this confidence toward God"* (I John 3:19-21).

*"By this we **know** that we abide in Him, and He in us, because He has given us of His Spirit"* (I John 4:13).

*"By this we **know** that we love the children of God, when we love God, and keep His commandments.' For this is the love of God, that we keep His commandments. And His commandments are not burdensome"* (I John 5:2, 3).

In these two verses John weaves *faith, love,* and *obedience* all together. They exist mutually in a dynamic relationship as the genuine proof of love is obedience, so that genuine proof of faith is love!

*"And this is the testimony that God has given us eternal life, and this life is in His Son. He who has the Son has life; he who does not have the Son of God does not have life. These things I have written to you who believe in the name of the Son of God, that you may **know** that you have eternal life, and that you may continue to believe in the name of the Son of God"* (I John 5:11-13).

*We **know** that whoever is born of God does not sin; but he who has been born of God keeps himself [or herself] and the wicked one does not touch him* (v. 18).

*"We **know** that we are of God, and the world lies under the sway of the wicked one* (v. 19).

*And we **know** that the Son of God has come and has given us an understanding, that we may **know** Him who is true; and we are in Him who is true, in His Son Jesus Christ. This is the true God and eternal life* (v. 20).

These last three passages constitute the summation of the whole letter. They contain three concluding absolute truths, each of which is introduced by the phrase **we know.** The overriding idea here is that a proper relationship with God results in confidence of our position in Christ within a confused and hostile world.

John is also encouraging us to help fellow brothers and sisters who are straying; we can be the instruments God uses to restore them in the fellowship. John has just reminded his readers everywhere of the **true God** (v. 20).

It is very fitting that he closes by exhorting them [and us] to stay away from idols. The false beliefs and practices are the idols from which the readers are commanded to protect themselves.

The false teachers upheld the world's philosophy as superior to God's revelation as demonstrated in their perversion of basic Christian teaching (faith, love, and obedience (v. 21).

In closing this book, John again highlights the importance of adherence to the fundamentals of the faith. This is the doctrinal foundation, out of which comes love and obedience.

"We know that the Son of God is come, and has given us an understanding, that we may know *Him* that is true, and we are in Him that is the true, even the Son Jesus Christ. This is the true God, and eternal life" (1 John 5:20).

"Little children
keep
yourselves
from idols. Amen.

– I John 5:21

CHAPTER 8 REVIEW: BECAUSE WE ARE NOT THERE

1. Discuss the sole purpose of the church to draw people into Christ.
2. Discuss the similarities of our day with Noah's day and Lot's day.
3. Discuss the sin of the normal people's way of living. How do we handle the same situation in America today?
4. Discipleship is a way of life.
5. God places His children safe from destruction "in Christ."

CHAPTER NINE

A COUNTERCULTURAL OF GOOD

"Who is wise and understanding among you? Let him show by good conduct that his works is done in the meekness of wisdom" (James 3:13).

When local churches commit to living a countercultural life for the good of all; then, being countercultural in this sense is not only about addressing historical issues from a biblical perspective but also addressing current hot-button issues that require courageous faith to do so from the same biblical truth.

During the 1960's T-shirts blazoned with upside-down flags, broken crosses, or Jesus' name plastered across billboards, and rebellion against the establishment, but eventually the 60's went and so did "Woodstock" and the rest of the icons of that era. Many people whose names became known in nearly every household across America are totally forgotten. So went the revolution! They presented themselves as countercultural to all that represented morality and all authority. True to history, soon a countercultural arose to counter them, and bring back or retain those pillars of society they attempted to destroy.

ANCHORED

Before we start running around doing good, we must insure that we are foundationally anchored:

- First of all through acknowledging our own need to be healed and restored.
- Be restored through authentic regeneration, and anchored assuredly justified in Christ Jesus.

Here being countercultural means bringing the truth of the Gospel, righteousness, and fruitful living flourishing with life and relationships to the broader culture. This is not and individual pursuit but to be expressed as God intended in God-centered communities of faith where *all* believers are involved in loving and caring for one another. Give God all the glory and invite others to experience the same grace.

Christians and churches that live this way find that not only is their faith revived, but their collective impact in areas of influence is vastly increased. Vast research has also shown that the millennia feel they are an *essential* force of good in such communities of faith. This is the expected fruit of faithfully living in the truth of God's Word.

Shock waves

In Luke 10:30-37, Jesus framed up a picture of being countercultural in His parable of the Good Samaritan. He sent shock waves throughout when He told the parable in answer to the question, "Who is my neighbor?" He upset their thinking by telling a story of two men divided by:

- Race
- Religion
- Socio-economics
- Politics

In the parable He brought it all together when a man with the biblical truth of good came upon a man [a Jew] who had fallen among thieves and now near death was in dire need. He got off his donkey and immediately began to restore, and attend the wounds of the broken and disheveled man. The shock waves got furious when Jesus pointed out this man was a [Samaritan], in that society this is the last person one would expect to come to the aid of any Jew. Remember these people were outcasts, hated for all the reasons listed above. Are you ready for this?

In many instances the countercultural only lasts as long as its visionary leads it, because in most, so few people embrace the new ideas that the movement soon dies. The countercultural Christ brought was an all together new way of living to the world. If Jesus had just done miracles and boggled the minds of the people all would have ended at the Cross, just a footnote in history. The endurance of Jesus' message and work [counter to the culture] is still ongoing today through His true believers.

"The crowds were amazed at His teaching; for He was teaching them as one having authority, and not as their scribes" (Matthew 7:28-29). The scribes and Pharisees relied strictly on their own natural power and ability for interpretation of the Torah. Jesus being Spirit-filled spoke with an authority that gave people a desire to follow Him:

- He so inspired them that they made life commitments.
- They were willing to die for Him.
- They were transformed into spiritual men and women of valor by His authority and power.

The answer to biblical counterculture brought to individuals, churches, homes, schools, governments and the marketplace is positive transformation. Men and women who have a biblically based worldview know there is tremendous opportunity for transforming all of these entities by reestablishing them on rock-solid truths and principles of the kingdom of God. God has provided the ultimate source for understanding the necessary transformational change – the Holy Spirit and the Word of God!

God's agents of change

Throughout the New Testament we find themes on which the people of God are to *stand* as counter-agents of change. Notice the following examples:

- In the Sermon on the Mount Jesus tells His listeners, *"Let your light so shine before men, that they may see your good works and glorify your Father in heaven"* (Matthew 5:16).

- Paul refers to a counterculture of good often in his letters to the early churches. *"And do not be conformed to this world, but be transformed by the renewing of your mind, that you may prove what is that good and acceptable and perfect will of God"* (Romans 12:2).

- *"And we know that all things work together for good to those who love God, to those who are the called according to His purpose"* (Romans 8:28).

- *"The kingdom of God is not eating and drinking but righteousness and peace and joy in the Holy Spirit"* (Romans 14:17).

- *"The fruit of the Spirit is love, joy, peace, longsuffering, kindness, goodness, faithfulness, gentleness, self-control. Against such there is no law."* (Galatians 5:22-23).

- *"And let us not grow weary while doing good, for in due season we shall reap if we do not lose heart"* (Galatians 6:9).

We are God's counter-culture agents. He has made us a new creation in Christ Jesus, so we can do the many good things that He planned for the anti-Christian culture gone wild in which we *stand* today.

Lights of Christ

In and through Christ, we are to be agents of restoration, putting right the effects of a broken and disordered world. We have no real ability to be or to generate the light of Christ on our own. Jesus said, without Him we can do nothing! This means that good works done with wrong motives can still have a positive impact. The effect of a sumptuous meal on a hungry person does not depend on our motivation. James said,

"Every good gift and every perfect gift is from above, and comes down from the Father of lights, with whom there is no variation or shadow of turning" (James 1:17).

At the same time, when it comes to growing to maturity in discipleship [a light of Christ] in the world, motivation matters tremendously. If we are trying to "out shine" one another in acts of love and works:"

- For the sake of our own reputation, to make ourselves look good, to make people like us or to promote a positive personal appearance, we are getting good wrong!

- Our good works should cause others to praise and give God the glory.

- If our works are to try to make ourselves worthy of God's love, we are driving away people with faulty lights rather than drawing them to Christ.

The light of our good works and righteous life should be in response of selfless love toward others in thanks for Jesus' unconditional love and sacrifice for us.

COUNTERCULTURAL

When Christian communities commit to living an authentic faith, they are truly a counter culture for the common good. Being countercultural, in this definition goes further than the one offered in an earlier section. Here countercultural means living "the faith" once delivered to the saints (see Jude 3), a life lived that is orderly and right, abundant and generous, growing with life and relationships toward the wider culture. This life is best expressed in churches where believers love and care for one another and then, witness and invite others in to experience the same grace. *Countercultural* is the word which identifies more and more believers who are leaving many of the more progressive contemporary churches that are allowing inclusivity, political correctness, and other non-biblical attitudes to over ride true holiness and separation unto the Lord. We pray that as increasing numbers of people come into the knowledge of the truth, people will come into the understanding that being countercultural does not mean being vindictive or condemning in any way. And we must never forget – the church is God's idea, not ours!

Know the Truth

As a soldier, three pieces of equipment becomes so essential for your own survival that you protect them with your very life. The items are 1) your personal weapon, 2) your first aid pack, and 3) your compass. Just looking at the three you might think they are simply self-exclamatory. Many Christians treat the ways and things of God that way; and they miss His whole purpose never able to attain the abundant life that He promises all of His children.

We could compare the Word of God [the Holy Bible], with a compass; both are primarily designed for direction. Many of us can remember the Dime store model compass from our childhood. We learned something about compasses: *true north and magnetic north* and the needle would point to one or the other north, but which one?

1. True north is based on the actual geographical location of the North Pole and is a *constant*.

2. Magnetic north *shifts* because it is centered on the earth's magnetic field, arising from its metallic core, which is molten, seething with heat and its effects.

Here is the kicker, there can be as much as a five-hundred mile difference between true north and magnetic north. Maps are aligned with true north, but compasses rely on magnetic north. Map declination tables have to be worked out so that travelers don't miss their destinations. Though we have technically progressed to the GPS and other instruments, the principles remain. Certainly this illustrates the challenge and confusion faced by students in the public educational systems.

If they come from godly homes and Bible-believing churches they have been taught *true north* [biblical values and ethics]. But when they get to school, the only directional focus available is *magnetic north*. Since the authority of the Bible has been totally separated from public education, there is no declination legend because to secular educational philosophy, there is no authority of the Bible, *true north*, which is absolute and constant.

Most of America's children go through their entire educational cycle never hearing about true north, the Bible. As a result upon entering kindergarten and moving on through school to graduate level studies and beyond the needle moves further away from true north.

Counterfeit tolerance

True tolerance is the ability to acknowledge and permit other peoples' views – even though you don' agree. We've always had that one, but today a new definition of tolerance has emerged. A "counterfeit tolerance" which says, "We will tolerate you as long as your opinion falls within the parameters of what we consider acceptable."

Much of contemporary church under the guise of being open and tolerant is actually producing carnal Christians, locked into political correctness, and pseudo-tolerance. True tolerance according to God's plan begins with true repentance and the new birth from above. Then the young disciples are encouraged to examine all the claimants to truth and discern the genuine from the false through the *spiritual* application of true north which is [the Word of God working in tandem with the Holy Spirit], moral absolutes, and God's unchanging truth.

Anti-Christian sentiment has progressively grown bolder and stronger over the past five or six decades providing a growing division in what it means to be moral; as cultural counterfeit-tolerance becomes the cultural norm. What does this actually mean for Christians who participate in public life where counterfeit tolerance is applauded and true biblical tolerance is unpopular and considered bigoted, and ignorance to the biblically illiterate?

There are presently reports of some churches and Para ministries who are partnering with parents and offering special courses on history, science, culture, and many other topics taught from the perspective of the biblical worldview. Praise God!

The principle of the new tolerance is considered one of the key virtues and strategic tools of relativism. However, in this fallen world the church must insure that there are people who call their societies to higher standards of living. This is an urgent function of Bible-believing, kingdom-minded, God-fearing churches – who truly enter to worship and scatter to serve. These are the true Spiritually-gifted people of God equipped and serving faithfully in all spheres of life including the marketplace.

Assimilate or accommodate

The faith once delivered to the saints of Jude 3 is the faith of those who follow Christ. Our relationship with our Creator is reflected in our talk and our walk. Our faith demands a way of life that honors our King. Demonstrating allegiance to King Jesus and faithfully following Him, we *stand* in opposition to a culture that demands our loyalty. To yield to that loyalty requires compromise and assimilation.

The Apostle Peter declares, *"We must obey God rather than human beings"* (Acts 5:29 NIV). It seems some times by their actions too many pastors and churches choose to "go along to get along." Many of them make this choice knowing that true Christlikeness demands so much more! Daily we see the great divide amongst our local churches in America – will we assimilate or accommodate? The difference stands out among the hot cultural issues of the day:

Assimilation – means embracing the claims, concerns, and commitments of our dominant culture. This is the path of least resistance. While they are silent and refuse to stand on the issues many local churches are forfeiting their religious freedom. The atheists and humanists are growing bolder in local government offices and courthouses across the land promoting their antichrist agenda.

It is imperative that the local Black churches across the land step up to the plate and be counted; our people are ill-informed about many things. Today, just a few days into President Trump's first of four years, candidates on both sides of the isles are no doubt jockeying and aligning themselves to make a run at replacing him. Selecting public officials today goes much deeper than just party affiliations. The person, platforms and campaign promises says much more about the candidate.

At every level today many biblical moral issues are at stake; definitions of familiar words are being redefined, new catch phrases are being devised to deceive or sway you. In courthouses across this country we are seeing the fruition of a phrase coined some years back, in a famous criminal trial that has become a reality – that is "legal justice" versus "moral justice."

"When justice is decapitated and something can be legal but immoral, we know we have already killed the heart of what it means to be human."

– Ravi Zacharias

A major responsibility of the shepherd is vigilance [to keep a watchful spiritual eye] for the welfare of the flock; and always be ready to properly address any danger on the horizons. Only God employs capable protection through the Spirit and the Word; especially today when widespread opposition is designed and sent by a spiritual foe who is always attempting to contaminate and bind all kingdom of God initiatives. Alone all human detection and other efforts are useless.

Strangely, many churches are sinking deeper and deeper into a pseudo-religious Christianity in which the churches become more traditional with the substituted aim of preserving a traditional way of church and church life rather than the advancement of the kingdom of God that spans all cultures and national groups. Churches must cut loose from these pseudo ties that bind; and tie themselves up to anchors sunk deep into the Rock of sound doctrine, Jesus Christ!

Such churches should heed Paul's warning: "Beware lest anyone cheat you through philosophy and empty deceit, according to the traditions of men, according to the basic principles of the world, and not according to Christ" (Colossians 2:8).

Amid the furious turbulences the philosophies of men and empty deception abound today causing many to lose sight of sound doctrine; and choose the principles of the world rather than Christ.

Paul's advice to the church at Ephesus is as true today as 2000 years ago:

"And He Himself gave some to be apostles, some prophets, some evangelists, and some pastors and teachers, for the equipping of the saints for the work of ministry, for the edifying of the body of Christ, till we all come to the unity of the faith and of the knowledge of the Son of God, to a perfect man, to the measure of the stature of the fullness of Christ; that we should no longer be children, tossed to and fro and carried about with every wind of doctrine, by the trickery of men, in the cunning craftiness of deceitful plotting, but speaking the truth in love, may grow up in all things into Him who is the Head – Christ – from whom the whole body, joined and knit together by what every joint supplies, according to the effective working by which every part does its share, causes growth of the body for the edifying of itself in love" (Ephesians 4:11-16).

Being Countercultural for good

Accommodation – means you chose a *countercultural* way. The Christian's commitment to a different set of truths and manner of life knowingly put us at odds with the dominant culture. We live alongside those with whom we disagree; which is essential to maintaining a faithful Christian witness.

In Daniel 3 we find an excellent example in the three Hebrews, Shadrach, Meshach, and Abednego who were put in high positions of government in the province of Babylon, yet they refused to serve and worship the idol the king had set up (see Daniel 3:12). Notice:

- They were under a different worldview than the surrounding culture which manifested in their actions.
- Their lives stood in direct contrast to their peers.

- The social pressure for their assimilation was no match for the three Hebrews' faithfulness. They said no to the culture.

- Their bold stand for their God changed the future for the Babylonian captives (see Daniel 3:28-29).

Undoubtedly the three Hebrews like Daniel had been prepared in family and community prior to their exile for this appointed time. Our faith in God can sustain us in a similar opposition only if we are prepared at home and in our local churches. One of the worst things you can do in the church of the culture is to say that someone else is wrong.

One third of Americans say that anyone who believes that same-sex relationships are wrong is intolerant. Think about it – just for your believing that God's intention for sexuality does not include gay sex can get you thrown into the culture's fiery furnace.

Be faithful to God

Being faithful to God often demands that we express ideas that conflict with the majority of the culture's claims, concerns, and commitments. What Christians believe about sin, human purpose, identity and ultimate meaning of life is at odds with the beliefs of many others. But we can't sit down!

Listen, we are to receive a message from thousands of years ago, words separated from us by generations and continents, connected by a thin page of print:

For the sake of those who are hearing us:

- We must cross the gap and *bring* back the message once delivered to those ancient believers.

- We must hear them though *their* language is different than ours.

- We must understand them, though *their* culture is foreign to ours.

- We must faithfully deliver *their message,* though we have never been in their presence.

- This understanding and bringing the message back through biblical interpretation is the primary task of the preachers and teachers.

I have preached with an interpreter who through the Holy Spirit translated my thoughts that I brought from America to a particular foreign country. The interpreter had to listen carefully and speak faithfully.

You must allow the message once delivered to the saints to speak again to this generation. *But it must be the same message.* The connection must be kept clear.

I mentioned expository preaching earlier which is best suited here so that the primary message of the Scripture text comes through as the primary message of the sermon. A Christian sermon is even in its method, a picture of God's grace.

The Scriptures are "the Word of life" (see Philippians 2:16). Since faith comes by hearing God's Word (Romans 10:17). Preaching the Word of God must be absolutely central; since Christians rely heavily on God's

Word. Notice the central role played by the Word in the New Testament church:

- So they all ate and were filled (Mark 6:42).

- And with many other words he testified and exhorted them, saying, "Be saved from this perverse generation." Then those who gladly received his words were baptized; and that day about three thousand souls were added to them. And they continued steadfastly in the apostles doctrine and fellowship, in the breaking of bread and in prayers (Acts 2:41-42).

- Preach the word! Be ready in season and out of season. Convince, rebuke, exhort, with all longsuffering and teaching (2 Timothy 4:2).

Accommodating other people's views create difficult conversations. But speaking the truth in love and grace, holding to our convictions, and living countercultural will go a long way toward seeing *truth* prevail – even when our views don't align with everyone else's. We will end this chapter with a powerful quote from missiologist Darrel Guder:

In all of his relationships, Jesus broke through the boundaries of likes and dislikes, social proprietary and religious acceptability, that characterized Palestinian society in the first century. Incarnational witness, as it was practiced by Jesus, challenged the accepted patterns of interpersonal relationships and community formation. It began with Jesus' own roots in Galilee, which marked him as a man from the margins. He was not identified with the religiously prominent and respected circles of his day. He came "from the wrong side of the tracks" ..... His choice of disciples continued the pattern of incarnational reversion of the acceptable structures of society. He called people to follow him who were ritually unclean (fishermen), nationally suspect (publicans), and politically dubious (zealots). He demonstrated the revolutionary character of the in-breaking reign of God by reaching out and touching lepers, by conversing publicly with women, healing the children of Gentiles. Allowing prostitutes to touch him, and going to parties with acknowledged con men. The church he founded continued this revolutionary pattern of incarnational witness, although it struggled with the challenges it represented. The Jerusalem church had to be convinced that Samaritans could really become followers of Jesus. Philip was led to evangelize a eunuch, who could never have joined in the ritual worship of the Temple community in Jerusalem. ... From very early on, however, it was clear that the church was to challenge the world as a community in which there was "no longer Jew or Greek, slave or free, male and female; "for all of you are one in Christ Jesus" (Galatians 3:28).[20]

CHAPTER 9 REVIEW: A COUNTERCULTURAL FOR GOOD

1. Discuss Jesus' countercultural parable of the Good Samaritan.
2. Discuss the essentiality of the Holy Spirit and the Word of God in transformational change.
3. We are God's countercultural agents for restoration.
4. The faith of Jude 3 is best expressed in churches where believers love and care for one another, witness to and invite others to experience the same grace.
5. One of the shepherd's major responsibilities is vigilance and to warn the flock of impending dangers.

CHAPTER TEN

POWER FROM ON HIGH

"Behold, I send the Promise of My Father upon you; but tarry in the city of Jerusalem, until you are endued with power from on high" (Luke 24:49).

"But the Helper, the Holy Spirit, whom the Father will send in My name, He will teach you all things, and bring to your remembrance that I said to you" (John 14:26).

"But you shall receive power after the Holy Ghost has come upon you, and you shall be My witnesses ...." (Acts1:8).

Some of Satan's greatest successes in spiritual warfare among Christians are through the deception that the Holy Spirit is a force, or that he does not really exist or that He came on the Day of Pentecost and returned to heaven. Then to, many believe He exists, but because of fear don't care to know Him personally, mainly because of the behavior of some who claim to have Him.

By their actions it seems that many Christians believe that the New Testament consists of only five *pertinent* books: Matthew, Mark, Luke, John and Revelation – that is what I call pseudo-religious Christianity which leaves out the Book of Acts and the Epistles. In other words it leaves *out* Christ's present High Priestly role in heaven, the Holy Spirit, the Church and the life of love and holiness we are to live.

I believe these beliefs give rise to today's easy salvation through a so-called new or modern grace; which allows continued sin, going beyond the biblical "unmerited favor," forgiveness and mercy of the New Testament. If not careful it could lead people to believe that God owes them "money" and other "material goods."

THE TRINITY

True Christianity believes in one God in three persons: God the Father, God the Son, and God the Holy Spirit. These are three distinct persons, not just appearances of the one God revealed in different forms. The three members of the Trinity are co-existent and co-equal. It's impossible to be a Christian without believing that Jesus Christ is God. He said of Himself,

"Therefore I said to you that you will die in your sins; for if you do not believe that I am He, you will die in your sins" (John 8:24).

If you open your Bible to the first verse Genesis 1:1, you are met with plurality [*"In the beginning God"*]. The Hebrew word for God is *Elohim,* which is a plural noun (more than one). A little later in the chapter God said, *"Let Us make man in our image"* (Genesis 1:26). The three persons of the trinity were involved in the creation.

The Old Testament is the record of the "age of God the Father," though not exclusively. In the four gospels, God the Son is the predominant One. Here we get the account of His birth, life, miracles, crucifixion, resurrection and ascension. But the *present age* is the dispensation of God the Holy Spirit, the Lord Jesus said,

"And I pray the Father, and He shall give you another Comforter, that He may abide with you forever" (John 14:16).

Literally, this verse might be rendered, "That He may abide with you for the age."

Our Lord Himself said, "Lo, I am with you always, even unto the end of the age" (Matthew 28:20). It's important that we thoroughly understand what He meant: God the Holy Spirit, the other Comforter (that is, another of the same kind), *is here*. This is His age of work. Just before His ascension, our Lord said to the disciples,

"And behold, I send the promise, of My Father upon you; but tarry in the city of Jerusalem until you are endued with power from on high" (Luke 24:29).

On the Day of Pentecost that power from on high came to the waiting disciples in the <u>Person of the Holy Spirit</u>. It was then that God the Holy Spirit came *to indwell* believers and inaugurate His work for this age, a work that will continue until the Lord Jesus Christ returns.

PENTECOST HAS COME

Saint Augustine called the Day of Pentecost "the birthday of the Holy Spirit." Like the Lord Jesus existed before He ever was born in Bethlehem and laid in a manger, yet we call that day the day of His birth [God incarnate]. We know that *"In the beginning was the Word, and the Word was with God, and the Word was God"* (John 1:1). He entered the world in His official capacity as the "sinless sacrifice."

Likewise, the Holy Spirit existed before He came at Pentecost. He entered the world in His official capacity. <u>He came into the world to *indwell*</u> those who are "born again" – from above. Throughout the Old Testament, the Holy Spirit came *upon* men and women for service. At Pentecost, He came to take up His residence *in* all of the true people of the faith.

Christ's promise fulfilled

The fourteenth chapter of John contains the record of the Savior's promise of the Holy Spirit's *indwelling*. Jesus responded to a question asked by one of the disciples:

"Lord, how is it that you will manifest Yourself to us, and not to the world?" (John 14:22).

Jesus answered and said to Him, *"If anyone loves Me, he will keep My word; and My Father will love him, and we will come to him and make our home with him"* (John 14:23).

It is very important that we understand what is said here. The promise is *"We will ...... make our home with him [or her]."* The plural is used here. This means that the first two persons of the Godhead, the Father and the Son, *abides or lives* in the believer through the third person of the trinity, the Holy Spirit. Earlier the Lord said, "the Spirit of truth, whom the world cannot receive, because it *neither sees* Him *nor knows Him,* but you know Him, for He dwells with you and will be *in* you" (John 14:17).

"....But you know Him, for He dwells with you and will be *in* you" (John 14:17).

The experience of the disciples then was that the Spirit of truth is the source of truth and communicates these truths to those who are His (see v. 16; 16:12-15). Just as the coming of Christ was prophesied, so also was the coming of the Holy Spirit. He would then abide *in* them.

The Holy Spirit was not yet given. But when Christ had fulfilled the law and types, and when He was *glorified* and had taken His place at the right hand of the Father, the Holy Spirit came down to communicate the finished work of Christ both to the individual believer and corporately to His Church.

Once again I want to remind you that each of the persons of the Trinity exercised and earthly ministry dealing with humankind and redemption:

- Under the law – God the Father came down through Mount Sinai's cloud, and through the Shekinah glory cloud.

- When God the Son – came into the world teaching, suffering, dying, and rising again, He laid the foundation for the new dispensation of grace.

- Today, while God is calling out a people from among the nations for His name, God the Holy Spirit – is here regenerating, renewing, and sanctifying the Church, the body of Christ.

Truly, power from on high came on the Day of Pentecost in the person of the Holy Spirit and He has never left!

Old Testament prophecy fulfilled

Pentecost was the fulfillment of an Old Testament feast of the same name. The sacred calendar of redemption that God gave Israel is recorded in Leviticus 23. It tells of seven great religious celebrations held in Israel. Together, these celebrations picture the work of our Lord and Savior, Jesus Christ from His death on the cross, His resurrection from the dead to its culmination in His millennial reign here on the earth. Those great feasts, filled with types were initiated with the Passover. So the advent of the Holy Spirit to indwell believers is the fruition of the Old Testament feast of Pentecost.

God the Holy Spirit began His appointed work in the Upper Room. The womb of the Virgin Mary was the prepared body in which the Son of God moved. Likewise, those 120 believers in the Upper Room were the infant body into which the Holy Spirit moved. In Ephesians 2:20-22, the Apostle Paul said that:

"….. having been built on the foundation of the apostles and prophets, Jesus Christ Himself being the chief cornerstone. In whom the whole building, being fitted together, grows into a holy temple in the Lord, in whom you are also being built together for a dwelling place of God in the Spirit."

Every new believer is a new stone in Christ's temple, the church, Christ's body of believers. Christ's building of His church will not be complete until every person who will believe in Him has done so. The apostle Peter explains:

"The Lord is not slack concerning His promise, as some count slackness, but is longsuffering toward us, not willing that any should perish but that all should come to repentance" (see 2 Peter 3:9).

MIRACLES IN THE CHURCH

We can take other lessons from the early Church. Those people whom God used mightily had the full arsenal of God at their disposal. In different parts of the world we see people dying rather than bowing to Baal or some other idol today.

Even here in America God is calling many of His mature saints to minister in ungodly environments, especially those environments that are *openly* hostile to the gospel. They must be able to hear "what the Spirit is saying to the churches," just as much as those in the pulpit.

Finally, wherever God places a leader in a church, that person assumes a position in a line of ministers that stretches back to the apostles commissioned by Jesus. As a result, church leaders are not authorized to *reinvent* or *modify* their responsibilities or the nature of their calling. They are constrained by the teachings of Scripture and the example of those who have gone before them as to what they can believe, teach, and do.

There are patterns of ministry to which they must conform. These ministries to Christ and others are a blessing both to the leader and the church. Let's take the example of James 5:14-15 which says,

"Is any sick among you sick? Let him call for the elders of the church; and let them pray over him, anointing him with oil in the name of the Lord: And the prayer of faith shall save the sick, and the Lord shall raise him up ; and if he have committed sins, they shall be forgiven him." KJV

Isn't it amazing that God does not tell us to dial 911, call a doctor, friends or even our spouse – but He specifically says, "Call the elders of the church?" Why? Because, God has given the local church access to His power:

- Church leaders are able to call on that supernatural power of God to accomplish the miraculous.

- The church has benefits the average member does not have an opportunity to obtain. Jesus said, "Whatever you [the church] bind on earth will be bound in heaven, and whatever you loose on earth will be loosed in heaven.

- Again I tell you that, "if two of you on earth agree about anything you ask for, it will be done for you by My Father in heaven" (Matthew 18:18-19).

- The church has been given special access to the power and authority of God through the work of Jesus Christ. We find a parallel passage to this in 1 Corinthians 5:4-5:

"When you are assembled in the name of our Lord Jesus and I am with you in spirit, and the power of the Lord Jesus is present, hand this man over to Satan, so that the sinful nature may be destroyed and his spirit saved in the day of the Lord."

When the local church is faced with a situation where a Christian is made a slave to sin, and despite our best human efforts, and they refuse to repent the church has another supernatural resource [church discipline] available that individual Christians do not have. The passage in 1 Corinthians 5 above says the church has the authority to ask God to "hand someone over to Satan," so that he or she might experience enough pain and pressure that they will come to repentance. This authority and promise of Christ's power are not by any means given to *individuals* in this way.

Because the local church has the power to exercise the discipline of God on an individual, it is the church – and not just the individual leaders – that is able to do more to help a sinning brother or sister. We also find church discipline in Matthew 18:15-17 which says,

"Moreover if your brother sins against you, go tell him his fault between you and him alone. If he hears you, you have gained your brother. But if he will not hear, take with you one or two more, that by the mouth of two or three witnesses every word may be established. And if he refuses to hear them, tell it to the church. But if he refuses even to hear the church, let him be to you like a heathen, and a tax collector.

The goal of this prescription for church discipline is restoration:

Step 1: "go tell him his fault" privately. If successful you have gained your brother.

Step 2: if he remains impenitent, "take with you two or three witnesses to fulfill the *principle* of Deuteronomy 19:15 which states, "One witness shall not rise against a man concerning any iniquity or any sin that he commits; by the mouth of two or three witnesses the matter shall be established."

Step 3: If he still refuses to repent, the matter is to be reported to the whole church v.17 – so that *all* may lovingly pursue the brother's or sister's reconciliation.

Step 4: If step three fails, then the offender must be excommunicated. The idea is not just to punish the brother or sister nor is it to shun them completely, but to remove him or her as a detrimental influence from the fellowship of the church, and henceforth regard this individual as an evangelistic prospect rather than a brother or sister.

The authority and power that God gives to the local church makes all the difference in the world in many practical situations. There is a radical difference when seeking counsel within the church and without. The Christian counselor outside the church can be helpful, but at best they are simply offering advice, which the counselee can take or leave as he or she sees fit. But counseling that happens within the structure of the local church where the counselee is connected relationally and accountable to others in the church body, carries with it a level of authority and power.

The unique power and authority that God gives to the church, combined with the operation of the diversity of spiritual gifts in the body of Christ and exercised under the care and guidance of godly leaders enables us to accomplish more through the church than we could by ourselves or in any other group.

Each of the three aspects we have looked at: spiritual gifts, leadership, and the local church's unique access to God's authority and *supernatural* power of the Holy Spirit within, which has been given to the church by God so that we might be better equipped to accomplish our God-given mission.

CHAPTER 10 REVIEW: POWER FROM ON HIGH

1. Discuss the "new" grace movement.
2. Discuss the various theories concerning the Holy Spirit.
3. Discuss the millennia reign of Christ.
4. God, the Holy Spirit inaugurated His work for the age, a work that will continue until the Lord Jesus Christ returns for His Church.
5. Discuss the events and significance of the Day of Pentecost.

CHAPTER ELEVEN

THE MINISTRY OF
THE HOLY SPIRIT

"Nevertheless I tell you the truth; it is to your advantage that I go away; for if I do not go away, the Helper [the Holy Spirit] will not come to you. But if I depart I will send Him to you. And when He has come, He will convict the world of sin; and of righteousness, and of judgment; of sin, because they do not believe in Me; of righteousness, because I go to My Father and you see Me no more; of judgment, because the ruler of this world is judged" (John 16:7-11). Bracket is mine for emphasis.

The Holy Spirit is the third divine person of the eternal Godhead, co-equal, co-eternal, and co-existent with the Father and the Son (see Matthew 28:19; II Corinthians 13:14; I John 5:7, 8). He is the believer's *promised* helper in all areas of life. It is His ministry to convict, convince, and convert human beings as well as to reveal the Son and the Father to the believer.

Since the glorification of our Lord, Jesus Christ – the Holy Spirit in all His glorious operations is working through all who believe on the Father through the Son. That is why the present era is known as the age of the Holy Spirit. Many prefer to call the Book of the Acts of the Apostles – the Acts of the Holy Spirit.

From Genesis to Revelation, concerning both creation and redemption, the Holy Spirit is seen in operation. He is seen in Genesis 1:1-2 moving: "And the Spirit of God moved upon the face of the waters." Between these two books, the final mention of the Holy Spirit is seen in Revelation 22:17, "… the Spirit and the bride say, come."

The ministry of the Holy Spirit is one of the most important doctrines in the Word of God and is one of the most essential truths of redemption. Therefore, every believer should seek to know all he or she can of the person, ministry, and work of the Holy Spirit as revealed in the Scriptures. He is a divine Person, He is God indwelling the believer and working within the believer to fulfill the will and purpose of God.

THE HOLY SPIRIT A DIVINE PERSON

Again, it is of great importance that the believer comes to know, understand, appreciate and experience the person, work and ministry of the Holy Spirit in his or her life. He brings to the heart the revelation of the Father and the Son (see John 14:15-16). Fear, formalism, spiritual, and biblical ignorance have robbed the church of the necessity of the knowledge of these truths for completion of God's plan of redemption. How?

God desires to have a personal relationship with each one of us. Thus He Himself comes and lives within us through the person of the Holy Spirit. We *must know* the Spirit is our friend, our helper, our comforter, and our indweller. The believer has more than an "influence" living within him or her – the person of the Holy Spirit!

His personal titles

Personal titles given to the Holy Spirit also show that He is a Divine person. He is called "the Comforter" or "Advocate" (see John 14:16, 26; 15:26; 16:7). This same title is given to Jesus as a person, meaning "one who stands alongside" (John 14:26). Jesus speaks of the Holy Spirit as "another comforter." He came to be personally related to the disciples that Jesus was related to when He was on the earth.

The Holy Spirit came to be personally *in them* what Jesus was personally *to them*.

In God's plan, this present age has been given over to the ministry of the Holy Spirit. Notice the personal acts:

He performs

- The Spirit works (I Corinthians 12:1)
- The Spirit searches (I Corinthians 2:10)
- The Spirit speaks (Acts 13:2; Revelation 2:7)
- The Spirit testifies (John 15:26; Nehemiah 9:30)
- The Spirit bears witness (I John 5:6)
- The Spirit teaches (John 14:26)
- The Spirit instructs (Nehemiah 9:20)
- The Spirit reproves (John 16:8-11)
- The Spirit prays and makes intercession for us (Romans 8:26)
- The Spirit leads (Matthew 4:1)
- The Spirit guides the believer into all truth (John 16:13)
- The Spirit glorifies the Lord Jesus Christ (John 16:14)
- The Spirit brings about regeneration (John 3:5, 6)
- The Spirit strives with men [people] (Genesis 6:3)
- The Spirit reproves men [people] (John 16:8)
- The Spirit sends messengers from God (Isaiah 48:16)
- The Spirit calls men [people] into ministry (Acts 13:2; 20:28)
- The Spirit also imparts spiritual gifts to the members of the Body of Christ (I Corinthians 12:7-11)

He has personal feelings

- He can be grieved (Ephesians 4:30)
- He can be insulted (Hebrews 10:29)
- He can be lied to (Acts 5:3)
- He can be blasphemed (Matthew 12:31-32)
- He can be resisted (Acts 7:51)
- He can be tempted (Acts 6:9)
- He can be vexed (Isaiah 63:10)
- He can be quenched (I Thessalonians 5:19)

THE HOLY SPIRIT'S MINISTRY IN THE NEW TESTAMENT

The Holy Spirit is God indwelling the redeemed "in Christ" and working within them to fulfill the will of God.

Be filled with the Spirit

Perhaps the most important realization of the ministry of the Holy Spirit as it affects the *experience* of the individual believer is embedded in the word *"filling."* This is an *experience* of which the word points inward. This word is associated with the work of the Holy Spirit in the believer some 12 times in the New Testament. Christians who are familiar with the New Testament would automatically think of Ephesians 5:18, the key Bible verse on the truth of the filling of the Holy Spirit:

"And be not drunk with wine, in which is excess, but be filled with the Spirit."

Why did the apostle Paul command believers to *"be filled with the Spirit?"* Note how he contrasts being drunk with wine with being filled with the Spirit. The answer to the question does not lie in the contrast, but in the comparison.

A person drunk with wine is controlled by the wine within him or her. The results will show up in their acts in ways that are normally not natural to him or her. In a similar manner, the person who is filled with the Holy Spirit acts in ways that are unnatural to the old nature. Instead of selfishness there will be consideration of others, instead of greed there will be generosity. Since the person full of wine is under its control, so a person full of the Holy Spirit is under His control. In other words Paul was telling believers to be controlled by the Holy Spirit.

Continuing to note Paul's experience, filled with the Holy Spirit, he was given the gift of *spiritual discernment* to see that the evil sorcerer was actually empowered by Satan (Acts 13:7-9).

Discernment is the ability to step back from our culture, customs, experiences, and prejudices, and see the world as God sees it.

It is the ability to disconnect from the familiar and see issues from God's perspective. Without vision we are doomed to the values of our culture, as modified by personal experience. In I John 4:1, John wants us to know that unless we are controlled by the Holy Spirit one cannot *"test the spirits to see whether they are of God."*

We live in days of great deception. Satan continues to counterfeit the true and don't forget he can perform miracles. We need the sharp spiritual discernment made possible through the *indwelling, controlling* Holy Spirit. Like the disciples of old, we bear witness of the risen Christ:

- Filled with the Spirit we to will speak the Word of God with boldness (Acts 4:31).
- Filled with the Spirit we allow the Spirit to produce Christ-like character [fruit of the Spirit] in us (Galatians 5:22, 23).

But to be filled with the Spirit does not stop there Ephesians 5:18, is followed immediately by four manifestations found in the life that is placed under the control of the Spirit. There will be:

1. An outward expression of praise – *"Speaking to yourselves in psalms and hymns and spiritual songs"* (v. 19).
2. Inward expression – *"Singing and making melody in your heart to the Lord"* (v. 19).
3. A thankful heart – *"Giving thanks always for all things unto God and the Father in the name of our Lord Jesus Christ"* (v. 20).
4. An attitude of humble submission: *"Submitting yourselves to one another in the fear of the Lord"* (v. 21).

If you carefully read Ephesians 5 and 6, you will see that the filling of the Holy Spirit affects every area of life:

- The inner man (5:18-21)
- The marital life (5:22-25)
- The family life (6:1, 4)
- Employment (6:5)
- Employers (6:9)

Are you truly depending on the Spirit of God for your daily walk? If deep within your heart you know that God's Spirit does not dwell in you because you have never been born again, you do not have assurance that you belong to Christ. Right now, trust the Lord Jesus as your Savior. Ask Him to come into your heart, and receive this promise:

"But as many as received Him, to them gave He power to become the children of God, even to them that believe on His name" (John 1:12).

The moment you receive Christ, the Spirit of God comes to dwell in you and lead you into all truth. Now you can face life with assurance and hope.

It is the blessed and glorious privilege of all believers to have the conscious love, joy, peace and knowledge of the Holy Spirit within you!

The Old Testament prophets foretold a coming day when the Spirit would be poured out upon all flesh, Jews and Gentiles together (see Joel 2:28-29; Ezekiel 11:19; 36:26-27; Isaiah 44:3; Zechariah 10:1). This could only be fulfilled upon the foundation of the death, burial, resurrection, ascension and glorification of the Lord Jesus Christ.

It would be Christ's ministry to receive the fullness of the Spirit as the perfect Man, the Messiah of God – and then pour out the same Spirit upon all flesh and upon those who believe on Him unto eternal life. Upon the acceptance of the finished work of Christ on the cross, the believer will find available to him or her the gift of the Holy Spirit and come under His workings from regeneration to glorification (see Matthew 3:11; John 1:30-33; Romans 8:25-32).

The Lord Jesus is the pattern Son of God, the Example of the workings of the Spirit in human beings. The believer as a child of God and member of the Church should follow in His steps and come under the same workings of the Spirit (see 1 Peter 2:21; Romans 8:29).

The whole life of Jesus as the perfect Man was governed by the Holy Spirit. *If Jesus depended upon the Holy Spirit for everything*, how much more should the believer constantly do the same?

All that God has for us and desires to do in us will only be done by the operation of the Holy Spirit in our lives.

The Holy Spirit working in the believer

Therefore the *need* for believers individually and the church corporately is to open their hearts and seek the fullness of the Spirit working in them – follow the example of Christ:

- The new birth is brought about by the Spirit (John 3:5-6).
- The Spirit indwells the believer's spirit (Romans 8:9; 1 Corinthians 3:16; 6:17; 1 John 2:27).
- The Spirit gives assurance of salvation (Romans 8:16).
- The Spirit fills the believer with Himself (Acts 2:4; Ephesians 5:18).
- The Spirit speaks to the believer (Acts 8:29; 1 Timothy 4:1; Revelation 2:7, 11, 17, 29).
- The Spirit open's the believer's understanding to the things of God (1 Corinthians 2:12).
- The Spirit teaches the believer, and guides him or her into all truth (John 16:13; 1 John 2:27).
- The Spirit imparts life (John 6:63; II Corinthians 3:6).
- The Spirit brings about renewal (Titus 3:5).
- The Spirit strengthens the believer's inner being (Ephesians 3:16).
- The Spirit enables the believer to pray (Jude 20; Romans 8:26-28).
- The Spirit enables the believer to worship in spirit and in truth (John 4:23-24; Philippians 3:3; 1 Corinthians 14:15).
- The Spirit leads the believer (Romans 8:14).
- The Spirit enables the believer to put fleshly deeds to death (Romans 8:13).
- The Spirit produces Christlike character and fruit of the Spirit in the believer's life (Galatians 5:22, 23).
- The Spirit gives a calling to the believer for special service (Acts 13:2-4).
- The Spirit guides believers into their ministry (Acts 8:29; 16:6-7).
- The Spirit empowers the believer to witness (Acts 1:8).
- The Spirit imparts spiritual gifts to the believers as He wills (1 Corinthians 12:7-11).
- The Spirit will bring about the resurrection and immortality to the believers' bodies in the last day (Romans 8:11; 1 Corinthians 15:47-51; 1 Thessalonians 4:15-18).

Not only does the filling of the Spirit result in change in the inner man and the various relationships of life, but it also produces a desire to work for the Lord. If you and I are to effectively serve the Lord, it is imperative that we be controlled by the Holy Spirit. On the great day of the feast Jesus said, "He that believes on Me, as the Scripture has said, out of the heart shall flow rivers of living water. *But this He spoke of the Spirit*......." (John 7:38, 39).

The Holy Spirit is the river of living water in the life of the believer. There are a couple of ways of disabling a spring, clog it up at the inlet or the outlet with chunks of trash. Similarly we can grieve the Holy Spirit with the sinful trash of evil words, thoughts and actions. Or we can quench the Holy Spirit by disobedience to the voice of the Lord. Confess your sin to the Lord and claim the promise that, "He is faithful and just to forgive us our sins, and to cleanse us from all unrighteousness" (1 John 1:9).

The Holy Spirit working in the Church

The work of the Spirit is not only seen in the individual believer but also seen in the Church, the body of Christ. The coming of the Spirit to form the Church was foreshadowed in Israel in the Feast of Pentecost; just as the work of Christ was foreshadowed under the Feast of Passover (see Exodus 12; Leviticus 23; Acts 2:1-4).

The Holy Spirit is the CEO of the Godhead who came to earth to build the Church that the Lord Jesus said He would build (see Matthew 16:16-20). The Holy Spirit could not *be given* until Jesus Christ was glorified after His death, burial, resurrection and ascension (see John 7:38-39).

The indwelling work of the Spirit has proven to be the *difference* between the experience of the Old and New Testament saints. Many church leaders are spiritually blind to the fact that the Holy Spirit and His gifts and ministries are the distinguishing features of the New Testament Church.

In the Old Testament the Holy Spirit descended on *chosen men of God*, equipping and filling them, but not indwelling them permanently:

1. The Spirit *"came upon me"* (see Judges 6:34; I Chronicles 12:18).

2. The Spirit came *"mightily upon"* men (see Judges 14:6; 1 Samuel 10:10; 16:13).
3. The Spirit was *"in men"* in the sense of indwelling at times (see Genesis 41:38; Numbers 27:18; Daniel 4:8-8; Nehemiah 9:30; I Peter 1:10-11).
4. The Spirit *"filled men"* equipping them for service (see Exodus 31:1-7).
5. The Spirit was often *"upon men"* (see Numbers 11:17; 24:2; Judges 3:10; 11:29; II Chronicles 15:1; Isaiah 59:21; 61:1).
6. The Spirit *"rested upon"* men (see Numbers 11:25-26; II Kings 2:15; Isaiah 11:2).
7. The Spirit *"moved upon"* men (see Judges 13:25).
8. The Spirit *"entered into"* men at times (see Ezekiel 2:2; 3:24).

To prevent any confusion, it should be remembered that these expressions of the Holy Spirit's coming only happened to chosen men of God, a chosen few whom the Spirit equipped for divine service.

The Promise fulfilled

Jesus *promised* His disciples that the Spirit would come and dwell *with* them and *in* them as the Comforter, He would abide with them forever (see John 14:16-17).

- The Holy Spirit formed the Church on the Day of Pentecost into a corporate structure on the streets of Jerusalem. He baptized the living members setting them into their places as stones in the New Covenant temple (see 1 Corinthians 3:16, 6:16; Ephesians 2:20-23; 1 Corinthians 12:12-13).
- Pentecost is called the birthday of the Church (see Acts 2:1-4; 1 Corinthians 12:12-27; Ephesians 1:22-23).
- The Holy Spirit brings anointing, illumination, direction and government to the Church as the New Covenant Priestly Body (see II Corinthians 1:21; Psalm 133:1-2; 1 John 2:20, 27; Ephesians 1:17-18; Acts 10:38; 1 Corinthians 12:12-13).
- The Holy Spirit brings gifts and graces to the members of the Church [spiritual gifts will be fully developed in Chapter 12] (see Ephesians 4:11-17; 1 Corinthians 12:12-13; Romans 1:6-8; Galatians 5:22-23).

- The Lord Jesus is the Head of the Church in heaven and He directs His affairs in His Body, the Church, through the Holy Spirit.

Just as Jesus Christ, the Head of the Body was under the total control of the Holy Spirit, and the Spirit was able to flow freely in perfect and unhindered operation, so this is to be manifested in the Church as the visible and mystical Body of Christ in the earth.

Right now Christ is seated in heaven. But the Bible tells us that mysteriously, He is present here on earth by His Spirit in the church, His body, which makes Him visible to the world.

Much is negatively said today about the church, God is not blind to the sins of the church individually or corporately. No matter how disappointed we are over the poorly crafted sermons, when our hard-earned money is wasted or misappropriated, what must God be thinking? Consider the seven local churches that Jesus confronted in Revelation 2-3. One has let their love for God grow cold, another is spiritually dead, another is filled with immorality and yet another is filled with idolatry.

Yet God refuses to abandon the church; though many people are ready to walk away from it, wow! What grace. God's continued acceptance of His church, despite our repeated offenses and failures, is one of the ways in which we reveal the love of God to the world.

The Holy Spirit working in the world

The work of the Holy Spirit is summarized clearly in John 16:9-11. The Holy Spirit has come with a three-fold ministry in relation to the world; to reprove the world of sin, righteousness, and judgment:

1. **Of sin** – because they believe not on Christ. Unbelief is the mother of all other sins. This area of conviction especially deals with the sin of a person.
2. **Of righteousness** – because Jesus Christ has gone to the Father. This area of conviction involves the righteousness of Christ, as the Savior of human-beings.
3. **Of judgment** – because the prince of this world, Satan, was judged at Calvary. This area of conviction involves the judgment of Satan and his hosts and their defeat at Calvary.

ATTRIBUTES AND MINISTRY

There are numerous names and titles of the Father and the Son in the Scripture; likewise for the Holy Spirit, particularly the essential and moral attributes of the Holy Spirit. Each of these attributes relate to some special need of human kind. All that is in God is brought to us by the Holy Spirit. He is all that we need:

- The Spirit of Wisdom (Isaiah 11:2; Ephesians 1:17)
- The Spirit of Knowledge (Isaiah 11:2)
- The Spirit of Counsel and Might (Isaiah 11:2)
- The Spirit of Grace and Supplications (Zechariah 12:10)
- The Spirit of Judgment (Isaiah 4:4)
- The Spirit of Burning (Isaiah 4:4)
- The Breath of the Almighty (Job 32:8; 33:4)
- The Spirit of Him who raised Jesus from the dead (Romans 8:11; 1 Peter 3:18).
- The Power of the Highest (Luke 1:35)
- The Eternal Spirit (Hebrews 9:14)
- The Spirit of Holiness (Romans 1:4)
- The Comforter (John 14:16, 26; 16:7)
- The Spirit of Love (II Corinthians 4:13)
- The Spirit of Truth (John 4:17; 16:13; 5:26; I John 4:6)
- The Spirit of Life (Romans 8:2; Revelation 11:11)
- The Spirit of Adoption (Romans 8:15)
- The Spirit of Faith (II Corinthians 4:13)
- The Spirit of Promise (Ephesians 1:3-4)
- The Spirit of Grace (Zechariah 12:10; Hebrews 10:29)
- The Spirit of Glory (I Peter 4:14)
- The Spirit of Power (II Timothy 1:7)
- The Spirit of Wisdom and Revelation (Ephesians 1:17)
- The Spirit of Prophecy (Revelation 19:10)
- The Good Spirit (Nehemiah 9:30; Psalm 143:10)
- The Free Spirit (Psalm 51:12)
- The Unction from the Holy One (I John 2:20)
- The Anointing which teaches us (I John 2:27)
- The Voice of the Lord (Ezekiel 1:24; Genesis 3:8; Isaiah 6:8)

We see the ministry of the Holy Spirit in the New Testament is all that of the Old Testament and more – for now the Spirit is for all people [all believers] out of every kindred, tongue, tribe and nation. The Holy Spirit not only "falls upon" (Acts 8:16; 10:44) is "poured out" (Acts 10:45); and "comes" (Acts 19:6).

The Holy Spirit now *indwells* the believer. That is, He came to remain and abide forever within the hearts of the redeemed.

This is the promise of the Father to the Son, and the promise of the Son to the believer.

Many theologians label the Book of Acts, the history of the church and rightly so; but the Book of Acts is also a continuation of the life of Christ – not on earth, but from heaven. Christ is the Head of the Church; which is His Body and He directs it through believers by the power of the Holy Spirit. Christ's mission is to the world! The Holy Spirit as the Spirit of promise brings all the promises of God to fulfillment in the redeemed community.

CHAPTER 11 REVIEW: THE MINISTRY OF THE HOLY SPIRIT

1. The ministry of the Holy Spirit is one of the most important doctrines in the Word of God.
2. He is a divine person, He is God indwelling the believer and working with the believer to fulfill the will and purpose of God.
3. Discuss the Spirit as our Advocate, Comforter, friend and helper.
4. The Spirit empowers the believer to witness for the Lord.
5. Carefully study Ephesians 5:18 and discuss the free flow and total control of the Holy Spirit in the life of Jesus Christ; and how this unhindered operation is to be manifested in the Church.

SECTION IV

WHERE DO WE GO FROM HERE?

CHAPTER TWELVE

THE EXERCISE OF
SPIRITUAL GIFTS

"But the manifestation of the Spirit is given to each one for the profit of all" (1 Corinthians 12:7).

"But one and the same Spirit works all these things, distributing to each one individually as He wills" (1 Corinthians 12:11).

We saw in the last chapter that without the indwelling Holy Spirit there can be no Christianity in the scriptural sense of the word, because there would be no true knowledge of God at all; one of the foundational works of the Holy Spirit is to usher us into the true knowledge and experience of God. Put another way, if there was no Holy Spirit, an encounter with God would be impossible, because the Spirit mediates the knowledge and thereby leads us into truth and righteousness (see John 16:5-11).

When we deliberately turn our hearts from the love of truth and redefine it to suit ourselves, we will experience the pseudo-fruit of our choices. Without the whole truth of the Holy Spirit and His ministries, many in the churches are being misled. They treat the Holy Spirit as if He is some kind of force or subjective feeling.

This belief and thinking stems from one thing, lack of biblical knowledge and failure to acknowledge the Holy Spirit. Others put all their emphasis on a particular gift or expression and hold to their outlook and concept of the Holy Spirit to the point that they can never imagine God blessing them in any other way. Quite often they even despise other believers who will not join them in their shouting or dancing. They may suggest that these other believers are not free in the Spirit; unthankful or in some instances, not saved?

Please understand I am not knocking any of these expressions or manifestations as being unscriptural. The Bible provides clear examples of all these things in the worship of God's people. Where the Spirit of the Lord is there is liberty to exercise this power. But it is unscriptural to suggest that any one of these expressions necessarily constitute true spiritual liberty.

LET YOUR LIGHT SHINE

Considering what has gone before, the question may be; how shall we know what to do, or when to do it? This is the office of the Holy Spirit, the sovereign Lord in the Church. He reveals and directs what to do, and when to do it. A local church that is directed by the Holy Spirit will do the right thing at the right time. He is the Source of all true liberty, harmony, and unity.

As I said in an earlier section, traditionally most Christians are use to the concept where one person leads the singing, one person prays, and one person preaches. Sometimes more than one of these activities may be combined in one person. Of the rest of the congregation little is expected – as they sit passively looking on. However, as we examine the life and worship of the church from the kingdom perspective as portrayed in the New Testament, we see active participation by all of the believers present in any service. This was initiated by the supernatural power of the Holy Spirit operating in and through the individual members.

A deeper study of this New Testament pattern reveals that the supernatural gifts and manifestations of the Holy Spirit are not given primarily to the individual believer. Rather they are given, through the individual believer to the church as a whole. Either way they cannot achieve their proper purpose; which is to grow the church numerically and mature it as the bride of Christ. The prescription for such growth and maturity is in the epistle to the Ephesians:

Speaking the truth in love, we will in all things grow up into Him who is the Head, that is, Christ. From Him the whole body, joined and held together by every supporting ligament, grows and builds itself up in love (Ephesians 4:15-16).

The Scriptures also say that *"to each one the manifestation of the Spirit is given for the common good"* (1 Corinthians 12:7), and *"each one should use whatever gift he has received to serve others"* (1 Peter 4:10).

- So the question is, "Are you a properly working part of the body of Christ?
- Are you a good steward of the manifestation of the Spirit that is given to you?

If the answer is no – what's hindering you? Is it sin, fear, procrastination, unbelief, insecurity, unworthy feelings, or just that you've been waiting for the Holy Spirit to move and do it Himself without your participation? Lay whatever it is before the Lord and say to Him, "Here am I Lord, with all my hesitations, and problems. Take me, and use Your gift through me to build your church. There sufficient documentation that the gifts of the Spirit, as well as one's natural gifts, can help the local church to grow.

Spiritual gifts are, of course, much more typical within the four walls of the church. But the effect of manifestation of Spiritual gifts outside of the church can be incredible. God's desire is that we let our light shine before all men. We certainly can't change the world when we are isolated from it. In fact we can validate the point:

The apostles performed many miraculous signs and wonders among the people ...... More and more men and women, believed in the Lord and were added to their number (Acts 5:12, 14).

Supernatural gifts

In 1 Corinthians 12, the Apostle Paul indicates how the gifts of the individual believers are intended to function within the corporate body. He said in v. 4, "There are diversities of gifts, but the same Spirit. There are differences of ministries, but the same Lord. And there are diversities of activities, but it is the same God who works all in all. But the manifestation of the Spirit is given to each one for *the profit of all:*

- To one is given the Word of **wisdom** through the Spirit
- To another the Word of **knowledge** through the Spirit
- To another **faith** by the same Spirit
- To another gifts of **healings** by the same Spirit
- To another workings of **miracles**
- To another **prophecy**
- To another discerning of **spirits**
- To another different kinds of **tongues**
- To another **interpretation** of tongues

But one and the same Spirit works all these things, distributing to each one individually as He wills (vv. 5-11). While stressing the diversity of gifts, Paul also stressed the singular source in the Spirit. This is the fifth mention in this chapter of the source of gifts being the Holy Spirit. It emphasizes that gifts are not something to seek, but to be received from the Spirit "as He wills." It is He alone who "works" or energizes (v. 6) all gifts as He chooses.

In verses 12-27, Paul goes on to say that the Christian Church is like one body with many members, and he likens each individual believer as a single member of the one body, ending with the words: *"Now you are the body of Christ, and members individually."*

Gift purpose

It is important to note that, though the spiritual gifts are given to individual believers, they are given to enable those believers to *fulfill* their proper part in the local church – to grow. Thus spiritual gifts are not intended primarily for the benefit of the individual but for the life and worship of the whole congregation. Luke validated this point:

"The apostles performed many miraculous signs and wonders among the people......More and more men and women believed in the Lord and were added to their number" (Acts 5:12, 14).

Through the manifestation of the gifts of the Spirit, the Jerusalem Church experienced phenomenal growth. Such responses to the gifts were not uncommon in those days; *nor should they be in ours.* God's purpose for the gifts is not only numerical, but also for maturing it as the bride of Christ. We find the prescription for such growth and maturity in the Epistle to the Ephesians:

"Speaking the truth in love, we will in all things grow up into Him who is the Head, that is, Christ. From Him the whole body, joined and held together by every supporting ligament, grows and builds itself up in love" (Ephesians 4:15-16).

The Scriptures also say that *"to each one the manifestation of the Spirit is given for the common good"* (1 Corinthians 12:7), and *"each one should use whatever gift he [or she] has received to serve others, faithfully administering God's grace in its various forms"* (1 Peter 4:10).

When the presence and power of the Holy Spirit are publically manifested through the various believers, the whole life and worship of the congregation are completely transformed.

Think about it the same Spirit who converts every believer – convicts every sinner. His purpose is to *"reprove the world of sin, and righteousness and of judgment"* (John 16:8). He manifests His will through the exercising of the gifts. The main responsibility for the ministry and the conduct of the service is no longer carried out by one or two believers while the remainder sits passive.

The goal is for every member of the church to actively participate in the service and to each other in the various member ministries; rather than one or two ministering all the time to all the rest.

Preparation for Service

In the Old Testament every detail concerning the service of tabernacle was taken care of by priests even down to the care, cleaning and maintaining of the utensils and all other equipment to include the altars and keeping the holy flame burning for fifteen hundred years. Their service was marked by **"lest ye die."** (KJV)

Ministry or service in the New Testament church is no exception. God gave the revelation to the apostle Paul, which he so ably describes for us as God's way of touching and changing the world. Paul turns to the provision made by the Holy Spirit for the church to be a dynamic and effective supernatural living organism functioning in the world but not of the world. Our service is marked by **"as unto the Lord."** He wrote, *"Grace was given to each of us according to the measure of Christ's gift"* (Ephesians 4:7).

From this brief passage we glean two clear points:

1. The gifts of the Holy Spirit are given to truly born again Christians for service.
2. The gifts are accompanied by a new supernatural manifestation of power with which to exercise them.

There seems to be no doubt that herein lays the starting point for the early church with their new converts. The new converts were immediately taught that the Holy Spirit had not only imparted into them, the life of Jesus Christ, but also had given them a spiritual gift or gifts which they are to discover and exercise. This is the pattern indicated by Paul's example of a body and it is confirmed by the words of Peter,

"As each one has received a gift, minister it to one another, as good stewards of the manifold grace of God. If anyone speaks, let him speak as the oracles of God. If anyone ministers, let him do it as with the ability which God supplies, that in all things God may be glorified through Jesus Christ"(1 Peter 4:10-11).

Peter speaks of God's manifold grace. That is it's so rich, so many-sided, that a different aspect can be manifested through each individual member in the total worship and service of God's people. In this way every member of the church may receive his or her own special manifestation and have something to minister in turn to all the other members. This picture of the church with every member active is confirmed by the words of Paul,

"For I say, through the grace given to me, to everyone who is among you, not to think of himself more highly than he ought to think, but to think soberly, as God has dealt to each one a measure of faith. For as we have many members in one body, but all members do not have the same function, so we, being many, are one body in Christ, and individually members of one another. Having then gifts differing according to the grace that is given to us, let us use them: if prophecy, let us prophecy in proportion to our faith; or ministry, let us use it in our ministering; he who teaches, in teaching; he who exhorts, in exhortation; he who gives, with liberality; he who leads, with diligence; he who shows mercy, with cheerfulness" (Romans 12:3-8).

Paul teaches that God has allotted to each member a special function, a special ministry. In conjunction with this, God has also made a double provision for the effective exercise of the ministry:

- The measure of faith
- The special gifts the ministry requires

Thus the New Testament picture of the church is a strong, active body of believers in which each individual member properly fulfills his or her special function. Paul describes the kind of service that is the result from this,

"How is it then, brethren? Whenever you come together, **each of you has** *a psalm, has a teaching, has a tongue, has a revelation, has an interpretation, let all things be done for edification"* (1 Corinthians 14:26).

That phrase "each of you has" sets a pattern; implying active participation by all the members to discover and operate in the gift or gifts you have been given by the Spirit. When Christians normally come together today, they do so with the primary purpose of:

- Receiving not of contributing
- Coming for a blessing not being or giving one
- Receiving healing
- Hearing the preacher

But this was not the way of the New Testament church. There the members came not primarily to receive but to contribute. Every one had something committed to him or her individually by the Holy Spirit to contribute to the total worship and service of the church.

Peter brings out the same point as Paul. The ability of the members to minister effectively to one another was due to the fact that they had received these supernatural gifts. They were therefore lifted out of the limitations of their own natural abilities of education, and talent into a much higher realm of spiritual freedom. When used properly, these gifts are quite effective in building up a local church.

They were able to fulfill as Peter says,

"As each one received a gift, minister it to one another" (1 Peter 4:10).

Only in the Spiritual realm

Why are so many professional ministers in our local churches suffering mental or nervous breakdowns? The answer is simply, that in many cases, one member is seeking to fulfill a ministry God intended to be divided up among all the members in the church. The only escape from the limitations and frustrations of this situation is through the supernatural ministry of the Holy Spirit in the church, dividing spiritual gifts to all the members individually, according to His own will.

Christians who think of spiritual gifts as sovereign acts of the Holy Spirit assume that the gifts operate without any corporation from human agents. On the other hand, there are those who still have an Old Testament mindset, and they assume that the Holy Spirit only uses a very select group for such demonstrations of His power. Again, a Spiritual gift is a specific capacity of function given to *each* Christian by the Holy Spirit as He sees fit. Its sad to say that most of the American church fail to understand that, as Joel prophesied, God would pour out His Spirit on all humankind, to both men and women, and that they would all move in the gifts of the Spirit (see Joel 2:28-32; Acts 2:17-18).

Still, there are also those who, after witnessing the operation of the Spirit, understand that God is co-laboring with people. Consequently, they are motivated to learn how to move in the gifts. Proper teaching will enable them to see beyond the splendor of the manifestations so that they may begin to understand the mechanics that cause the supernatural occurrences.

This delivers believers from their own natural limitations by lifting them into a spiritual realm where they can share the total ministry of the church. When all the members are equipped to function in their individual ministries the church as a whole can fulfill its corporate role as the body of Christ (prayerfully and carefully study Ephesians 4; I Corinthians 12; Romans 12; I Peter 4) for the gift listings and (I Corinthians 13-14) for the biblical-way of operating in the gifts.

THE GREATEST OF THESE IS LOVE

Among the various reasons for which God gives the gift of the Holy Spirit is the pouring out of divine love [agape] within the believer's heart (Romans 5:5) occupies a position of grave importance. Notice the gifts are given in Chapter 12 and their rules of engagement are given in Chapter 14; however to get to the rules of engagement, you must go through Chapter 13, the love chapter. For a deeper study on the Spiritual gifts and ministry see chapter 10, Subject: "When Power Comes to Church" in my book titled *A Light unto My Path*.[21]

The reason for that is, *without* the activating influence of divine love in the believer's heart all significance in the use of any spiritual gift will automatically fail to accomplish its true purpose; therefore, to emphasize the essential significance of this [*agape*] love – With deep humility, Paul uses a series of examples to emphasize the significance of *agape* love:

"Though I speak with the tongues of men and of angels, but have not love, I have become as sounding brass or a clanging cymbal. And though I have the gift of prophecy, and understand all mysteries and all knowledge, and though I have all faith, so that I could remove mountains, but have not love, I am nothing" (1 Corinthians 13:1-2).

First he considers exercising the gift of tongues on such an elevated supernatural level that he speaks not only unknown human tongues but even the language of angels. He says that if he were to do this *without* divine love, he would be no better than a gong or a cymbal that produces a loud noise when it is struck but is quite empty inside.

Then he considers the possibility of exercising other outstanding spiritual gifts – such as prophecy, or the word of wisdom, or the word of knowledge or faith. But he says that if he should exercise any or all of these gifts without divine love – he would be absolutely nothing.

These words of Paul provide the answer to a question asked by many today: "Is it possible to misuse the gifts of tongues?" Yes, it is possible to misuse the gift of tongues. Any use of tongues or any other spiritual gift *apart* from divine love is a far-reaching *misuse* of that gift. We hear many exclaim that if the person began to misuse God's gift, that God would withdraw the gift from him altogether.

However, a free gift, once given, passes out of the control of the giver and is thereafter under the sole control of the person who received it – whether to use, or abuse, or not to use at all. Scripture confirms this point of logic: *"For the gifts and the callings of God are irrevocable"* (Romans 11:29).

The word irrevocable used here of God, and not of man, indicates that once God has given a gift, He never takes it back. Thereafter the responsibility to make proper use of the gift rests not with God but with the receiver of the gift. This important principle applies in all areas of God's dealing with humankind.

The love test

There is only one sure, scriptural test of continuing fullness of the Holy Spirit, and that is the love test. In the measure that we are filled with the Holy Spirit – is the same measure we are filled with divine love. John applied this test clearly,

"Beloved, let us love [agape] one another, for love is of God; and everyone who loves is born of God and knows God. H who does not love does not know God, for God is love" (1 John 4:7-8).

Anyone who in any measure manifests this kind of love has in that measure, come to know God through the new birth. Any person who has never known or manifested this love in any measure has never known God, for in the measure that a person comes to know God, he or she is in that measure changed and transformed by the divine love, and begins to manifest it to others.

As John indicates, this manifestation of *agape* – of divine love – commences in human experience with the new birth from above. This is in agreement with the words of Peter:

"Since you have purified your souls in obeying the truth through the Spirit in sincere love of the brethren, love one another fervently with a pure heart, having been born again, not of corruptible seed but incorruptible, through the Word of God which lives and abides forever" (I Peter 1:22-23).

"In this love [agape] of God was manifested toward us, that God has sent His only begotten Son into the world, that we might live through Him" (1 John 4:9).

"No one has seen God at any time. If we love one another, God abides in us, and His love has been perfected in us. By this we know that we abide in Him, and He in us ..... God is love, and he who abides in love abides in God, and God in him" (1 John 4:12-13, 16).

Five reasons Christians love

The Old Testament and the New Testament are the sole standards by which all teaching is to be tested. In 1 John 4:7-21, John constitutes one long unit describing what perfect love is and that it is available to humankind. In this discussion He introduces the reader to five reasons why Christians love:

1. Christians love because God is love (4:7, 8)
2. Christians love to follow the supreme example of God's sacrificial love in sending His Son for us (4:9)
3. Christians love because love is the heart of Christian witness (4:12)
4. Christians love because love is the Christian's assurance (4:13-16)
5. Christians love because love is Christian's confidence in judgment (4:17-20)

One cannot love God without first loving his fellowman. John is not talking about sinless perfection, but rather mature love marked by confidence in the face of judgment. Confidence is a sign that love is mature. The love that builds confidence also banishes fears. We love God and reverence Him, but we do not love God and come to Him in love, and at the same time, hide from Him in terror (see Romans 8:14, 15; 2 Timothy 1:7).

CHAPTER 12 REVIEW: SPIRITUAL GIFTS AND MINISTRY

1. Discuss what happens to an individual or church who fails to acknowledge the Holy Spirit as the sovereign Lord of the Church.
2. The Holy Spirit is the Source of all true liberty, harmony, and unity in the church.
3. Discuss Spiritual gifts given by the Holy Spirit to individual Christians in the church.
4. The same Holy Spirit that convicts sinners is the same Holy Spirit that converts sinners.
5. Discuss the series of examples the apostle Paul uses to emphasize the significance of agape love in I Corinthians 13.

CHAPTER THIRTEEN

GOD'S END STRATEGY

"Till we all come to the unity of the faith and of the knowledge of the Son of God, to a perfect man, to the measure of the stature of the fullness of Christ; that we should no longer be children, tossed to and fro and carried about with every wind and doctrine, by the trickery of men, in the cunning craftiness of deceitful plotting, but speaking the truth in love, may grow up in all things into Him who is the head, Christ from whom the whole body joined and knit together by what every joint supplies, according to the effective working by which every part does its share, causes growth of the body for the edifying of itself in love" (Ephesians 4:13-16).

What is God's end and goal through the church? What is the end of it all? We now come to the text above, where we find the apostle Paul's great statement of the end and goal of all God's expansive strategy for all of humankind. God's end goal strategy is not the evangelization of the world. The Great Commission is more often than not held up to us as the supreme goal and purpose of the church and is truly a crucial task.

Notice in the Scripture at hand twice Paul gives us the ultimate goal of the life of faith; which is the yardstick by which we can measure our progress as Christians:

1. In verse 13 he says it is *"the measure of the stature of the fullness of Christ.*
2. And in verse 15 he urges all believers to *"grow up in every way unto Him who is the Head [into Christ].*

Here referring to the body of revealed truth that constitutes Christian teaching particularly featuring the complete content of the gospel. Oneness and harmony can only be realized among believers only when it is built on the foundation of sound doctrine. Paul is not referring to salvation knowledge, per se, but to the deep knowledge of Christ that a believer comes to have through prayer, faithful study of His Word and obedience to His commands (see Philippians 3:8-10, 12; Colossians 1:9, 10; 2:2). The above goals are totally impossible without the Spirit and the Word working within us.

Indicating also that God wants each believer individually and corporately to fulfill our humanity, according to His designed plan for us all that He intended when He created the first man and the first woman.

We stated earlier that evangelization of the whole world is not God's ultimate purpose in the local church. Certainly, Christ commanded us to preach the gospel to every creature – but by His criteria. We are told specifically in Romans 8:29 that God's ultimate plan for all believers is that we be *"conformed to the image of His Son."*

Evangelism is a means of bringing people into a relationship with God through proclaiming the truth in love – so that His ultimate goal for them – Christlikeness – can be achieved in their lives. God wants every believer to manifest the qualities of His Son who is Himself the standard for their spiritual maturity and perfection.

Biblical church growth

Christ gives us power through the Holy Spirit within for our becoming mature, equipped believers – not through our own efforts, but from our Head, the Lord Jesus Christ. Godly biblical church growth results from every member of the body fully engaged and using his or her spiritual gifts in submission to the Holy Spirit and in fellowship with other believers (see Colossians 2:19). Spiritual and biblical immature believers who are not grounded in the knowledge of Christ through the truths of God's Word are:

1. Inclined to uncritically accept every sort of demonic doctrinal error.
2. Accept fallacious interpretation of Scripture bought about through deceitful false teachers in the local churches.
3. Easy prey for the devil to plant strongholds in our thinking [mind]; in many cases they were passed on in our childhood – the Spirit and the Word of God transforms our disposition [outlook].

Christ our Example demonstrated how to handle all three of these critical conditions as He *in the Spirit* wielded *the Word of God*, dealing with Satan in the wilderness. Satan strove with Him through temptation in all points "as we are, yet without sin," (carefully study, Matthew 4:1-10; Hebrews 4:15; 1 John 2:16):

• The "lust of the flesh" (vv. 2, 3)
• The "lust of the eyes" (vv. 8, 9)
• The "pride of life" (vv. 5, 6).

As it is written

All three of Jesus' replies to the devil were taken from Deuteronomy. It is true that Jesus was tempted like as we are, and He overcame every temptation without sinning, He was born, lived and died, *"without sin."* He was made to be sin, yet He knew no sin (II Corinthians 5:21). He "did not sin, neither was guile found in His mouth" (I Peter 2:22).

• In His birth He was called "that Holy One" (Luke 1:5).
• In His childhood He was most extraordinary and superior.
• In His adulthood He asked His enemies, "Which one of you convinces Me of sin?"
• The temptations of Jesus were from *without,* not from *within.*
• We are tempted and drawn away of our own lust (James 1:14).
• Our temptations come from *within* as well as from *without,* but not so with our great High Priest.
• On every occasion, Jesus answered Satan with the Word of God:

"Man does not live by bread alone."
"Thou shall not tempt the Lord your God."

"Thou shalt worship the Lord thy God and Him only shalt thou serve." KJV

Throughout the temptations, there was no doubt in Satan's mind who Jesus was, but his strategy was aimed at getting Jesus to violate the plan and strategy of God by employing the divine power that He had set aside in His humiliation (see Philippians 2:7).

Preparation for ministry

We see Jesus' preparation for this event even back when at the age of 12, taking the role of a student listening and asking questions; He was able to speak to the teachers in the temple with wisdom and authority of the Scripture, putting them to shame (see Luke 2:46). The question may be asked, "Why was the sinless Son of God baptized?" In his "Expository Outlines on the New Testament," Dr. Warren Wiersbe suggests six reasons:

1. Obligation – "to fulfill all righteousness" (cf. John 8:29).

2. Consecration – The Old Testament priest was washed. Jesus submitted to baptism, then anointed. The Holy Spirit came as a dove (Matthew 3:16).

3. Commendation – Jesus approved of John the Baptist's ministry, while the religious leaders rejected his baptism (Matthew 21:23-27).

4. Proclamation – John's official introduction of Jesus to the Jewish nation (John 1:31).

5. Anticipation – this baptism looked forward to His baptism of suffering for us on Calvary (Luke 12:50).

6. Identification – Jesus identified Himself with sinful humankind (see Leviticus 16:1-10).[22]

Discernment of spirits

In review let's remember the spiritual gifts are listed in 1 Corinthians 12; while the operations of the gifts are recorded in chapter 14. However, to get from the gift listing in chapter 12 to the operation of the gift in chapter 14, you must pass through Chapter 13 and agape [sacrificial love].

First Corinthians 14:3 describes how God used His Word, given through New Testament prophets, to minister to the spiritual needs of the people. It is imperative that they are able to discern spirits.

Discernment enables one to perceive immediately whether or not a person who supposedly was exercising the gift of prophecy or any other gift are speaking or operating by the inspiration of the Holy Spirit. With prophecies being regularly given in churches and with many false prophets and false teachers around giving their demonic messages – there was then and there is the need for immediate *discernment* between true and false revelations today.

The apostle John admonishes that we, *"Do not believe every spirit, but test the spirits, whether they are of God; because many false prophets have gone out into the world. By this you know the Spirit of God: Every spirit that confesses that Jesus Christ has come in the flesh is of God, and every spirit that does not confess that Jesus Christ has come in the flesh is not of God. And this is the spirit of the Antichrist, which you have heard was coming, and is now already in the world"* (I John 4:1-3).

Knowing that his time is short, Satan has intensified his attacks against the people of God, the Church. His demons counterfeit God's message and work. It is essential to have people in the church who are discerning. They are as I stated in an earlier section, the guardians, and the watchmen who protect the church from demonic lies, false doctrines, perversions, and fleshly elements.

To effectively operate in this gift requires diligent, study of the Word to exercise gifts of knowledge, wisdom, preaching and teaching, so it does with discernment.

In 1 Thessalonians 5:21-22, Paul says, "Test all things; hold fast what is good. Abstain from every form of evil." Then again in Acts 20:30, He warns, "Also from among yourselves men will rise up, speaking perverse things, to draw away the disciples after themselves. Therefore watch, and remember that for three years I did not cease to warn everyone night and day with tears."

Two threats are always present to the church, one from the outside and one from the inside:

1. Unbelievers are a constant threat from the outside.
2. The arrogant, narcissists are a threat from within.

Contentious and divisive people cause a snare which can cause others to stumble – causing strife and divisions and destroying the peace and unity of the church. Paul says such people should be avoided. Through the wisdom and obedience of believers, God will crush this work of Satan in the church.

In Romans 16:17-18 He admonishes, "Now I urge you brethren, note those who cause divisions and offenses, contrary to the doctrines which you learned, and *avoid* them. For those who are such do not serve our Lord Jesus Christ, but their own belly and by smooth words and flattering speech deceive the hearts of the simple." Ultimately, God will totally defeat Satan and bring peace to the entire church.

CHAPTER 13 REVIEW: GOD'S END STRATEGY

1. Discuss the importance of every convert being taught that the Great Commission is not the supreme goal of God's salvation, but His goal is the conforming each believer to the image of His Son.

2. Discuss Paul's prescription for the deep knowledge of Christ: 1) prayer, 2) faithful study of God's Word, 3) obedience to His commands.

3. Discuss Christ's standard for the believer's maturity and perfection.

4. Discuss the 3 dangers that the immature believer lacking in spiritual and biblical knowledge recorded in chapter 13 of this book.

5. Discuss Paul's advice concerning the snare of those who's contentious and divisive behavior hinders in the local church.

CHAPTER FOURTEEN

HOW WE GOT HERE

"Though we walk in the flesh, we do not war according to the flesh. For the weapons of our warfare are not carnal but mighty in God for pulling down strongholds" (II Corinthians 10:3-4).

This portion of Scripture, chapter 10 is very practical and timely. Paul's general design here is to vindicate his apostolic authority. As Christians, we should be exceedingly grateful for the great lessons we learn from Paul's attitude regarding his *unpleasant experiences* with the church at Corinth. I think that we are living in a time when many of our local pastors are going to have to admit that the path they are carrying their churches down is not the correct path.

ARE THE TARES IN CHARGE?

Anyone can praise God and be a happy Christian when things are going well and people are saying kind things – but when enemies attack and slander, then real Christian character and grace is manifested. If a person is really spiritual, he or she will be a true Christian even when things are unpleasant; proving that God's grace is sufficient for every trial.

Paul had ministered for a long time in the city of Corinth. For eighteen months he had worked, prayed and labored with his own hands as a tentmaker to support himself and those with him while he preached publicly and privately, from house to house, attempting to reach every lost sinner he could for Christ.

Here is a lesson for today's local churches – Paul continued to labor with them after they were saved so that *each* believer might grow in grace and the knowledge of our Lord and Savior, Jesus Christ. Under his tutelage and pastoral leadership the work grew, and developed in a very gracious way. After proper leadership was developed, Paul moved on to other fields, that he might sow the seed of the Gospel to those who had heard the glorious message of the saving grace of God.

In his absence from the church in Corinth, Paul was made aware that there was an undercurrent, created by the enemies of the Gospel of the grace of God, intent upon turning Paul's own converts away from him causing them to lose confidence and respect for him as an inspired apostle, ordained of God. Paul knew that the demonic intention of these enemies of the Gospel was to undermine and weaken the faith of the converts, and other true believers alike in the church. And cause them to be limited as they declared the gospel of the saving grace of God which he had preached unto them. The Corinthian believers would not be effective witnesses if they listened to these enemies of the finished work of Jesus Christ.

THE HOUR FOR ACTION IS COME

At this juncture the Apostle Paul had to insist strongly upon the authority that the Holy Spirit had given Him. He had to *defend* his apostleship, because he knew God had made him an apostle. He was the apostle to the Gentiles and as such he magnified his office.

Like the apostle Paul the time had come for him to exercise severe discipline unless they changed their attitude. You have accused me of being governed by worldly motives and worldly policies. This is untrue; and unless you change your mind and repent in your heart, I shall be compelled to us decisive measures because of your improper conduct (see vv. 3-6).

These verses certainly imply that there may be times when believers, especially pastors and other leaders of the church will be required to lay aside the meekness and humility which Christ usually manifested, and to assert themselves and act with authority and severity. On occasion Jesus did just that as seen in the record in [John 2:13-16].

Today is such a time when pastors and other Church leaders, like Paul, must assert themselves and act with authority and severity to bring the American Church back to the biblical standards of the New Testament and the faith of Jude 3, which was once delivered to the saints.

Many of our pastors, teachers and other Christian leaders seem oblivious of what is happening in the local churches today. Pluralism is alive and working hard at turning Christians from a Godly biblical worldview to a cultural secular worldview.

NO COMMAND STRUCTURE

Having served in the U.S. Army, a Vietnam War veteran, and retiring after 26 ½ years of active service; I know quite a bit about secular command structures. I think that one of the greatest hindrances in the local churches in America is churches trying to derive and exercise Christian authority from the same *source* as secular or worldly authority does. The world's view of authority places a person over another, as in a military command structure, a business executive hierarchy, or a governmental system – certainly as it should be.

Demanded by the competitiveness created by the fall of humanity which resulted in the rebelliousness and ruthlessness of sinful human nature – the world would not be able to function without the use these of command structures.

The *source* of authority for secular humanism and atheism is *experience, science* and *reason*. The fates of many local churches are hanging in the balance as they attempt to function *through* the world's source of authority!

But Jesus clearly stated, **"It shall not be so among you."** Emphasis added throughout. Disciples are in a *different* relationship to one another – than those of the world outside of the church. Christians are:

- brothers and sisters,
- children of one Father
- members of one another in the body of Christ

Jesus made the point very clear in Matthew 23:8, *"You have one teacher, and you are all brethren."* Sad to say the church has rejected or ignored these words of Jesus for the past twenty centuries. So it has repeatedly borrowed the authority structures of the world. Please remember the world structures do not believe that God or the supernatural exists.

In most churches today, an unthinkable acceptance has been given to the idea that the pastor is the final authority in both doctrine and practice, and he or she is the Chief executive officer of the church with respect to administration. But if the church *is not* to imitate the world in this matter, what is it to do? Again, the question is answered in Jesus' words, **"You have one teacher."** Emphasis added.

I have heard it repeated in several quarters that some of the founding fathers of this nation were Deists [who believed that God created everything, but left the world to feign for itself].

True or false, many of the American churches have behaved for centuries as if Jesus is far away in heaven having left it up to church leaders to make *their own* decisions and run *their own* affairs. I'd say that makes then at least "practical deists," don't you agree?

Christ's vision of church leadership

Scripturally, we have to agree that most of what we see of church leadership in America is far different than what Jesus assured the disciples in the Great Commission, **"Lo, I am with you always, even to the end of the age."** And in Matthew 18:20, He reiterated, **"Where two or three are gathered in My name, there am I in the midst of them."** Do we get the picture?

It is quite clear that Jesus, Himself is present in the Holy Spirit not only in the church as a whole, but in the local churches as well. It is Jesus Christ Himself who is the *ultimate authority* within every local body of Christians through His representative the Holy Spirit.

The task of human leadership is *not* to run the church themselves but determine through the leading of the Spirit and the Word of truth, Christ's will for running His church. A through study of Scriptures clearly made much of this known including the impartation of spiritual gifts and the enablement of the indwelling Holy Spirit. He also made clear through the Spirit and the Word the responsibilities of the believers to:

- Bear one another's burdens
- Confess their sin's to one another
- To teach, to admonish, and to encourage one another
- To hold one another accountable
- And to evangelize and serve the needs of a hurting world

Without a doubt, the "one another" ministries in the body of Christ are very important to God, since He speaks of them so frequently In His Word. Prompting the question, "What provision is made by the churches to encourage it and guide its practical expression through scriptural teaching and admonitions?

Small group ministry

In the early church, as we see it described in the New Testament, Christians gathered together mainly in homes to instruct one another, study and pray together, and share in the ministry of spiritual gifts. Then they would go out into the marketplace to let the warmth of their love-filled lives overflow into Spirit-filled Christian witness that drew many love-starved pagans into the church.

In many local churches today you can find some expression of small group ministry taking place in private gatherings in Christian homes. Of course the group and sponsoring church leadership must be in agreement otherwise the "small group" would be branded a trying to divide the church. This type of ministry doesn't threaten the unity of the church; actually it is the very thing the church is supposed to be about according to the New Testament.

This is in line with the exhortation of Jesus to His disciples:

"A new commandment I give to you, that you love one another; even as I have loved you, that you also love one another. By this all men will know that you are my disciples, if you have love for one another" (John 13:34-35).

A two-fold witness

The early church flourished upon a two-fold witness as the means of reaching an unbelieving world: *kerygma* [proclamation] and *koinonia* [fellowship]. It was the combination of these two that made the church's witness so powerful and effective. *"In the mouth of two or three witnesses shall every word be established"* (Matthew 18:16).

To bear one another's burdens at the very least means to uphold one another in prayer.

Pagans of that day could easily shrug off the proclamation as just another "teaching," but it was much more difficult to reject the evidence of fellowship. The concern of Christians for each other, and the way they *shared their lives* in the same family of God – left the pagan world craving this new experience called koinonia. A pagan writer remarked: "How these Christians love one another!"

Koinonia calls for honesty and openness with other Christians, and a mutual recognition that is neither abnormal nor unscriptural to have burdens and problems in our day-to-day Christian experience. The psychotic masks must come off – that claims "that everything is all right" – when everything is not all right! Stop masking truth!

The present day church has almost done away with true New Testament koinonia; which completely, reduces the witness of the church to only proclamation [preaching]; this does two things that simultaneously causes great harm:

- Removes the major safeguard to the health [doctrinal truth] of the church corporately and individually from *within*.
- Greatly weakens the churches effective witness individually and corporately before the world *without*.

It is no wonder, that the church from within and the world from without has fallen on evil days and is regarded as irrelevant and useless by so many people. The church is too busy:

- We must get back to spending time with another person so that *you* can thoroughly understand that person's feelings and problems.
- It means committing yourself to an authentic effort offering prayer, practical help, or wise counsel —not just "I'll pray for you."
- Many Christians see other Christians in need and pride themselves as being a "practical" referral agent, well, that's what the Red Cross is for," or "that's why we have an unemployment office," "that's the very reason I pay taxes."

Referral agencies such as the Red Cross, Salvation Army and government entitlement programs can be welcomed help – but none of these agencies can take the Christian's place of caring, expressed through an act of love, a word of encouragement, or when prayer is needed.

- People need to hear other Christians who have the same kinds of problems.
- They need to see their problems in others.

The story is told of Frederick the Great, King of Prussia on a tour of the Berlin prison during the mid-1700s, as he entered the lower dungeon about a dozen prisoners fell on their knees before him. "Have mercy on us, Your Majesty!" they pleaded. "We are innocent! We have been falsely imprisoned. Are all of you innocent? "Yes!" they insisted.

Then King Frederick noticed a man who quietly stood over in a dark corner of the dungeon, "You there," said the king, "Why are you in this prison?" "I was convicted of armed robbery, Your Majesty, Guilty and ashamed. I deserve to be in this place."

King Frederick called the Guards! See that man in the corner? Take him out of here and release him at once!" Then he pointed to the dozen men who had claimed to be unjustly imprisoned, and said, *"I will not have these fine, innocent men corrupted by one guilty wretch!"*

We are like that guilty prisoner. It is not our façade of goodness, but *the honest confession of our sin* that sets us free! We are challenged in James 5:16, "Confess your faults to one another and pray for one another, that you may be healed. The prayer of a righteous man [or woman] has great power in its effects." Emphasis added.

CHAPTER 14 REVIEW: HOW WE GOT HERE

1. If a person is really spiritual, he or she will be a true Christian even when things are unpleasant, proving that God's grace is sufficient for every trial.
2. Discuss the occasion in which Paul had to insist strongly upon the authority that the Holy Spirit had given him. On occasion pastors and other church leaders may be required to assert themselves and act with authority and severity.
3. Discuss the difference of relationships to one another in the church with those of the world outside.
4. Discuss the benefits of koinonia operating in the local churches.
5. Discuss Christians in their place of caring expressed through an act of love and encouragement; also being there when prayer is needed.

CHAPTER FIFTEEN

THERE IS A WAY OUT!

"If anyone comes to Me and does not hate his father and mother, wife and children, brothers, and sisters, yes, and his own life also he cannot be my disciple. So likewise, whoever of you does not forsake all that he has cannot be My disciple" (Luke 14:26, 33).

There are many people who think that getting saved from sin is simply a means of getting to heaven when they die. They go about their lives as though they belonged to themselves and feel absolutely no obligation to the Lord and His work in the world.

To trust in the Savior for salvation is to assume the obligations of being the Lord's disciple. After He saves us, the Lord Jesus begins to show us the need for discipleship, which is essential to Christian life and ministry.

"And as He walked by the Sea of Galilee, He saw Simon and Andrew his brother casting a net into the sea; for they were fishermen. Then Jesus said to them, "Follow Me, and I will make you become "fishers of men." They immediately left their nets and followed Him" (Mark 1:16-18).

Jesus called fishermen, hardworking and industrious people, to perform the most important task on earth – being fishers of men [a lifetime calling].

THE REQUIREMENTS OF DISCIPLESHIP

A disciple then is a pupil, or a learner. *Their supreme goal is to become like their teacher* (see Matthew 10:24-25). The ultimate goal of each believer is to be Christlike.

True disciples of Jesus not only receive His teachings and walk in His fellowship – but also pass on His teachings to others extending His kingdom influence in the world:

- Discipleship is a *spiritual discipline* that is to continue throughout the life of *all* gospel believers.
- Discipleship is *required* for Christian life and ministry.

One cannot be a disciple of Jesus without paying the cost. This cost is the requirement of discipleship for all. Consider the cost:

1. Our forsaking all for Christ (Luke 14:26, 33)
2. Our taking up the cross (Luke 14:27a)
3. Our following the Lord Jesus (Luke 14:27b)

The Lord gave His followers three parables that show the need for their fulfilling the requirements of discipleship:

1. Jesus warns of the possibility of being ridiculed by the world for not [*counting the cost*] and therefore not being able to complete the requirements of discipleship. Following Christ is not something to be sought on a trial basis – but calls for an ultimate commitment (see Luke 14:28-30).

2. The Lord pointed out the foolishness of making a shallow commitment to discipleship without counting the cost (see Luke 14:31-32).

3. The Lord pointed out "the loss of saltiness" brings the undesirable results of not fulfilling the requirements of discipleship (see Luke 14:34-35).

We hear much today concerning modern grace and fresh grace; which in many cases is just a repackaging of the old "once saved always saved" and therefore you can continue in sin because Jesus has already taken care of it for you. God forbid!

In the parables above Jesus warned that an ineffective commitment leads to being *cast* aside. This is apparently referring to:

Those Christians who are judged to be unfaithful – Paul clearly says in 1 Corinthians 11:30, they could face an untimely death, a punishment suffered by some Christians who failed to *examine* themselves at the Lord's Supper (also see 15:18; 1 Thessalonians 4:15, 16).

In Luke 9:62, Jesus said, *"No one, having put his hand to the plow, and looking back, is fit for the kingdom of God."*

This remark by Jesus concerning our being fit for the kingdom of God demonstrates the seriousness of commitment to Him. The call of God should take preeminence over everything else. Distractions and over-looking through the rearview mirror can cause you to veer off the path [task].

THE WAY OUT [TRUTH]

Although it may seem contrary to our experience, we who are saved are no longer related to sin as we once were. To avoid unnecessary grief and irreparable loss and to live holy and victorious lives – God has *revealed* the truth for us to learn. To better understand the believer's relation to original sin, we must first look at our new relation to the Lord Jesus Christ, which undergirds *His truth.*

The believer's relation to the Lord Jesus Christ

The apostle Paul declared that, for new believers, the old things have passed away and all things are now new (2 Corinthians 5:17). At salvation, we believers were severed from Adam's family and joined to the family of God – in Christ. Being "in Christ," we have everything new, including our sharing in:

- The Lord's divine nature and the prospect of one day His kind of body (see Philippians 3:20-21).
- His obedience unto death and the blessed results there of (see Romans 5:17-19).
- And His death and resurrection (Romans 6:3-4).
- The new life with Christ we are no longer related to original sin as we once knew it.

The believer's changed relation to original sin

We have seen that unsaved people have an active relation to original sin and its effects. They possess a corrupted personhood and human nature – dominated by the sins of the flesh, being spiritually dead, morally defiled and guilty before God. However, now "born again from above," their relationship to original sin is drastically changed.

1. The true believers are divinely forgiven of all sins, original and actual imputed sin and guilt (Ephesians 1:7; Colossians 2:13).

2. The true believers are now justified by God (Romans 5:1, 9; 8:30, 33; Titus 3:7). If we were still guilty of original sin, we could not be righteous (justified) now. In fact, we *cannot* now be successfully charged with or condemned judicially for any sin because of the atoning work of Jesus Christ our Lord and Savior (Romans 8:34; Hebrews 7:25).

3. Sadly, many Christian churches believe that water baptism washes away imputed sin and guilt – this is not the correct teaching of Scripture. However, it is *eternally important* to believe and accept by faith that our original sin and guilt, and actual sin were washed away by the precious blood of Jesus' atoning sacrifice in response to the true believer's faith in Jesus as his or her Savior (Romans 3:21-25; Ephesians 1:7; Hebrews 9:26; Revelation 1:5).

4. The true believers are inwardly delivered from inherited sin and corruption. With the deliverance of our personhoods, souls, and spirits, from inherited corruption – *now saved, we are capable of understanding spiritual truth, expressing our emotions, and make right moral decisions.* Because of this, we can now worship and serve God with our spirit and soul (see Philippians 3:3; Romans 1:9; 1 Corinthians 14:15).Although our personhoods and souls are renewed and our spirits saved and delivered from hereditary corruption, they are still susceptible demonic influences. The Apostle Peter wrote about "fleshly lusts, which war against the soul" (see 1 Peter 2:11).

5. True believers are made spiritually alive. The believer's personhood, and having partaken of Christ's divine nature received eternal life and he or she was made spiritually alive (see John 3:16; 6:47; Ephesians 2:1). This new life springs out of a new, personal relationship with God (John 17:3) that true believers enter when they are born into God's family (John 1:12) and they became citizens of His kingdom (John 3:3-6; Colossians 1:13). This new life is communicated to God's people by the Holy Spirit (see Romans 8:2; Galatians 5:25). He also provides the dynamics for their interacting with God and for their displaying Christlikeness in daily life. It is our duty to yield our total being, spirit, soul and body to the will of the indwelling Holy Spirit (Romans 12:1; and to allow Him to produce His holy fruit in our lives (Galatians 5:16, 22-23). He keeps our spiritual enemies in check as well as help us to do what is pleasing in the sight of God (Galatians 5:16; James 4:7; Romans 8:2-4).

We died to sin (Romans 6:1-14)

The apostle Paul argued that where sin abounds more grace abounds (Romans 5:20), then it seems logical to keep on living in sin (Romans 6:1). But the apostle Paul answered with a resounding, NO! (v.2). How can people who have died to sin continue to live in it? Since our bodies are still unredeemed sin is still present. Paul clearly brought this out in (Romans 6-7; also see I John 1:8).

Although we are still able to sin, we no longer have to give in to sin's demands because of the radical changes in our relation to sin when we were saved. We died to sin and were delivered from its authority. We are now alive unto God and we are the property of the Lord Jesus Christ and definitely subject to His authority (see Romans 14:8-9; 1 Corinthians 6:20; Matthew 11:28-30).

Know truth

Because of our baptism [placement] into Christ at salvation (Galatians 3:27), spiritually speaking we died with Him, thus we died to sin (vv. 3, 6; 1 Peter 2:24). We were also buried with Him (Romans 6:4a). Finally, we arose with Him; thus, we are alive unto God (Romans 6:4b, 5). This truth affects us in two ways:
1. We do not have to sin (Romans 6:6-7).
2. We are now alive to God to do His will (8-10).

Upon activating the principle that we have died unto sin and are now alive unto God (v. 8; Galatians 2:20), the apostle sees an analogy of this *truth* with our Lord's physical experience of death and resurrection (Romans 6:5, 9-10). Notice, as Jesus' resurrection cut death's grip on Him, so our death with Him has cut our relation to sin and our resurrection with Him has made us alive unto God. Now we can "walk in newness of life" (v. 4).

Think about it, our being dead to sin and being alive to God to be true (v. 11):

- We must respond to this *truth* by a decision and action in a corresponding way (vv. 12-13).
- That is to stop giving ourselves to the *demands* of sin and to start giving ourselves fully to God as His instruments of right being and doing.
- We have liberty to make this decision and to act upon it at anytime (I Peter 2:16; Galatians 5:13).

Victory over sin

I say then, *"Walk in the Spirit, and you shall not fulfill the lust of the flesh. For the flesh lusts against the Spirit, and the Spirit against the flesh; and these are contrary to one another, so that you do not the things that you wish"*(Galatians 5:16-17).

You may be asking, "What is the lust of the flesh?" *The lust of the flesh is any kind of selfish, fleshly desire.* The greatest problem in the life of the majority of Christians is how to avoid living selfishly – how to be victorious over selfish desires. The text answers that question clearly: *"Walk in the Spirit."* If we:

- Walk by the Holy Spirit.
- Are led by the Holy Spirit.
- Yield ourselves fully to the Holy Spirit.
- Present our bodies a living sacrifice holy and acceptable unto God.
- Give the Holy Spirit right of way in our lives.

He will give us the victory over our selfish, lustful desires. I say again, as I've said throughout in the writing of this book, "There is much ignorance among Christians concerning our relationship as believers to the Holy Spirit. I know it will be advantageous to stop here and once again point out a few important points concerning that relationship:

1. Every person who is a recipient of God's grace – is born of the Holy Spirit and through the power of the Holy Spirit becomes a child of God (see John 3:3-8; James 1:18; 1Peter 1:22; 2:3).

2. The moment the new birth is experienced, the love of God is poured out in that person's heart and the Holy Spirit is given to them (see Romans 5:5).

3. Every born again child of God should be and can be filled with the Holy Spirit. When the born again one is filled with the Holy Spirit he or she will walk in the Spirit, and not fulfill the lusts of the flesh. The command here in Ephesians 5:18 is, *"Be filled with the Spirit,"* That is a continuous action.

But if you are led by the Spirit, you are not under the law. Now the works of the flesh are evident which are:

- Adultery
- Fornication
- Uncleanness

- Lewdness
- Idolatry
- Sorcery
- Hatred
- Contentions
- Jealousies
- Outbursts of wrath
- Selfish ambitions
- Dissensions
- Heresies
- Envy
- Murders
- Drunkenness
- Revelries

"And the like; of which I tell you beforehand, just as I also told you in time past, that those who practice such things will not inherit the kingdom of God" (Galatians 5:18-21).

It would not be wise for me to waste paper and ink to try to enlarge on what the Holy Spirit tells us through the apostle Paul. They will not be in the number when the saints go marching in except they repent and turn to Christ for forgiveness. Paul said in I Corinthians 6:9-11, as he listed these same sins of the flesh as in Galatians 5:18-21, "And such were some of you. But you were washed, but you were sanctified, but you were justified in the name of the Lord Jesus and by the Spirit of our God."

This list of works of the flesh does not pertain to blood-washed believers because they are not characteristic in the lives of born again, redeemed Christians (see I Corinthians 1:29-30).

Born again believers, those who are Christ's, have crucified the flesh with its passions and lusts. It is Christ whom we have put on by faith, therefore we say with Paul,

"I am crucified with Christ: nevertheless I live; yet not I, but Christ lives in me: and the life which I now live in the flesh I live by the faith of the Son of God, who loved me, and gave Himself for me" (Galatians 2:20).

"If we live in the Spirit – let us also walk in the Spirit" (v. 25).

That is, if we are born again of the Spirit, if the Holy Spirit abides within us, then let us yield ourselves to Him ...... and let us give Him the right-of-way in our lives – in every minute detail of our life. The Holy Spirit is not a dictator. He will not do for us or through us, more than we allow Him to.

POWER TO WITNESS

Christ Himself points out the results of the indwelling Holy Spirit in two passages where He gives final instructions to His disciples before His ascension into Heaven:

"Behold, I send the Promise of My Father upon you; but tarry in the city of Jerusalem until you are endued with power from on high" (Luke 24:49).

"But you will receive power when the Holy Spirit has come upon you; and you shall be witnesses to Me in Jerusalem, and in Judea and Samaria, and to the end of the earth" (Acts 1:8).

In these two verses Jesus give His outline plan for the spread of the gospel in this present age. This simple outline contains three-stages:

1. Each believer [New Testament priest] is to be personally empowered by the Holy Spirit.

2. Each believer, empowered by the Spirit, is by personal testimony to win others to Christ.

3. These others [that are won] are empowered by the Spirit to win yet others.

In this manner the testimony of Christ will be extended outward from Jerusalem in ever-widening circles of power until it has reached the end of the earth [all nations and all creatures]. Whenever this plan is applied it will always work – meaning it makes possible the evangelization of the entire world in any century in which the church puts the plan to work. There is no alternative plan that can offer the same results.

Power and Authority

The Greek word used for "power" in the Scriptural verses above is *"dunamis"* from which we get the words *dynamo, dynamic,* and *dynamite.* The impression given from these English derivative words is that of a forceful, explosive impact. In the passage below the primary concept is associated with the new birth from above is "authority."

"But as many as received Him [Christ], to them He gave the "right" to become children of God" (John 1:12).

Again this verse describes the new birth. The Greek word translated "the right" is *exousia.* "Exousia" denotes a nature derived from some external source. So, the person who receives Christ as Savior receives, in Christ, the nature of God. Thus the receiver of this new nature from God produces within the new birth.

The English word most commonly used to translate *"exousia"* is *"authority."* This is the distinctive mark of the born-again child of God. He or she is no longer a slave to sin, but now a son of God and possessing *a new authority.* He or she no longer falls into temptation, but meets and overcomes these things by virtue of the new nature by the Spirit of God within. He or she is an overcomer and now has authority. Please know that power and authority are not the same.

The power of His Presence

It is imperative that we notice, the first disciples had this authority from the time of Christ's resurrection onward. They were already "sons of God." They were already capable of leading godly overcoming lives. While they were no longer slaves to Satan and sin, during the period between the resurrection and Day of Pentecost these first disciples made little impact on the inhabitants of Jerusalem.

All of that quickly came to a halt and dramatically changed however, by the descent of the Holy Spirit on the Day of Pentecost. As soon as the 120 believers in the upper room were baptized in the Holy Spirit – the whole of Jerusalem was impacted. Within a couple of hours thousands had gathered and before the day ended three thousand unbelievers were converted, baptized and added to the church. Undoubtedly the adding of *power* to *authority* produced these glorious results.

After Pentecost they had the power needed to make their authority fully effective. The evidence and outworking of this new supernatural power was very apparent in the Book of Acts, notice the passages below:

"And they were all filled with the Holy Spirit, and they spoke the word of God with boldness" (Acts 4:31).

"And with great power the apostles gave witness to the resurrection of the Lord Jesus" (Acts 4:33).

"The high priest complained to the apostles: And look, you have filled Jerusalem with your doctrine" (Acts 5:28).

Everywhere the early Christians presented the testimony of the resurrection of Christ in the power of the Holy Spirit; the impact on the populace was tremendous.
* In Samaria: "And there was great joy in the city" (Acts 8:8).
* In the city of Antioch in Pisidia: "And the next Sabbath almost the whole city came together to hear the Word of God" (Acts 13:44).

In the city of Philippi the enemies of the gospel complained of Paul and Silas:

* "These men, being Jews, exceedingly trouble our city" (Acts 16:20).

In Thessalonica the enemies of the gospel said of Paul and Silas:

* "These who have turned the world upside down have come here too" (Acts 17:6).

As a result of the opposition to Paul's preaching in Ephesus:

* "The whole city was filled with confusion" (Acts 19:29).

Christian Witness then and Now

One consistent feature marked the effectiveness of the early Churches' witness in every place and that was "a mighty spiritual impact upon the whole community." Throughout their travels there was either a revival or a riot; sometimes both together. Two noticeable things that could not survive in the wake of the great impact of the gospel of Christ: ignorance and apathy.

Today the conduct and experience of Christians have almost executed a one hundred and eighty degree turn-around. This is happening even to many groups of Christians who have truly experienced the new birth:

- They attend church regularly for worship
- They lead decent very respectable lives
- They cause no trouble
- They cause no riots

Lest we forget, the church is called to make Jesus *visible to the world* in the same manner that Jesus made *the Father visible:* by being *full of grace.* However, today most churches make little or no impact. In the community all around them, Spiritual and biblical illiteracy, and indifference concerning other spiritual things abound everywhere unchanged, and unchallenged. The majority of their neighbors neither know nor care to know what these Christians believe or even why they attend church. What is missing? Power!

The Christian church as a whole needs to face up to Paul's challenge in 1 Corinthians 4:20, *"For the kingdom of God is not in word but in power."* Jesus tells us that God will give the Holy Spirit, His indwelling presence, to those who ask.

Sadly, we hear so little about this today. The greatest need in the church today and in the individual Christian *is the indwelling presence of God,* the Holy Spirit. Many who know of Him keep Him at such a distance because that is where the local churches have put Him. Then when we are in need and call on Him in prayer, we wonder where He is. He is exactly where we left Him!

In Revelation 2:1-7, John alludes to this condition as present in the church of Ephesus. Ephesus was one of the urban cities in the Roman Empire, very similar to our own cities of rich and poor, intellectuals and unlearned and a rallying place for many pseudo-religious groups and superstitions. The Ephesus church was a dynamic group that persevered through troubled times.

When Paul moved into Ephesus to declare war on the forces of darkness, he did not preach a series of sermons on the evils of Diana [the idol goddess], nor did he preach "Do not bow at the shrine of Diana." Wherever he preached his single subject was: *"God forbid that I should glory, save in the cross"* and as always Paul was determined not to know anything except Jesus Christ and Him crucified.

The Holy Spirit used Paul mightily to break the power of darkness and lead converts against the terrible systems of idolatry (see Acts 19). Church discipline was very prevalent in the church at Ephesus, a leading model for others. The epidemic of "false apostles" that we have in the local churches of this country would not be tolerated in the church at Ephesus. They carefully scrutinized visiting ministers to ensure their authenticity.

They also despised the Nicolaitans, a sect which led a narcissistic and immoral life. Those who counterfeit and distort the purity of biblical truth are to be fervently countered by true love for God. Though this church had many commendations of dedication, patient, disciplined and discerning, Jesus saw through the pious façade. *"Yet I hold this against you: you have left your first love"* (Revelation 3:4).

The Ephesians had lost their love for Christ and each other. I have counseled many couples whose claim by one or the other "I just don't love her or him anymore." Love should increase not decrease. What happened to the girl whose heart sped up just being in his presence? Where is the man who used to bring flowers and tell her how fortunate he was to have met her?

Similarly, across this country today we find church buildings which are involved in "good works" out of tradition or a sense of duty. This is shocking when the one for whom their love is lost is the Lord of glory – it is time to tremble and fall upon our knees when the Lord holds – the loss of love against the church.

Once the diagnosis has been made, the prescription plan can be written. Christ gave us a three point plan to renewing love:

1) **Remember** – what it was like in the beginning. Relive the thrill of romance, the desire to tell the world how sweet it is to be married to her. In the case of the Christian remember the joy of having accepted Jesus Christ as Savior and Lord. Remember?

2) **Repent** – turn your life around. Make a conscious commitment to get the relationship right again.

3) **Return** – "do the first works" those acts of love, even if you don't feel like it. Do it the feelings are secondary.

Christ ends every one of His letters to the churches with the same conclusion: *"He who has an ear, let him hear what the Spirit says to the churches"* (Revelation 2:7). In our busy everyday affairs of daily life; we may allow our love relationship with the Lord to grow weak. The church at Ephesus warns us all: the Lord is to have first priority in our lives.

LOVE IS THE HEART OF CHRISTIANITY!

When a church or an individual departs from the virgin love of the new birth experience, that person or church will find itself slipping farther and farther as the days and weeks go by. The glory of Ephesus had departed and the once proud heathen city, the capital of idolatry, today is a "poor, miserable village" – known as *"Ayasalook."*

The heart of Christianity

Yes, the believers in the Church at Ephesus were hard workers. They labored in patience, they hated evil, but in spite of that the Lord had something against them. Revealed in this condemnation is the *root* of church and individual failure: **Departure from Christ!**

We learn from the New Testament record that only what we do because we love Jesus with all our heart, soul and strength will receive a reward in the end. "....... We should do all to the glory of God." I will conclude this chapter with that passage praying that we all carefully examine ourselves and the local churches in the light of it:

"To the angel of the church of Ephesus write, These things says He who holds the seven stars in His right hand, who walks in the midst of the seven golden lampstands: I know your works, your labor, your patience, and that you cannot bear those who are evil. And you have tested those who say they are apostles and are not, and have found them liars, and you have persevered and

have patience, and have labored for My name's sake and have not become weary. Nevertheless I have this against you, that you have left your first love. Remember therefore from where you have fallen; repent and do the first works, or else I will come to you quickly and remove your lampstand from its place – unless you repent. But this you have, that you hate the deeds of the Nicolaitans, which I also hate. He who has an ear, let him hear what the Spirit says to the churches. To him who overcomes I will give to eat from the tree of life, which is in the midst of the Paradise of God" (Revelation 2:1-7).

CHAPTER 15 REVIEW: THERE IS A WAY OUT

1. Discipleship is a spiritual discipline that is to continue throughout the life of all gospel believers.
2. Carefully review the three parables Jesus gave for fulfilling the requirements of discipleship on page 161.
3. At salvation, we believers were severed from Adam's family and joined to the family of God "in Christ." We have everything new. Carefully review what we have on page 162.
4. Discuss how we do not have to sin after being born again, because of radical changes in our relation to sin.
5. Discuss how we died to sin and were delivered from its authority.

SECTION V
GETTING IT RIGHT

CHAPTER SIXTEEN

APPROACHING THE KING OF GLORY!

"Most assuredly, I say to you, he who believes in Me, the works that I do he will do also; and greater works than these he will do, because I go to My Father. And whatever you ask in My name, that I will do, that the Father may be glorified in the Son. 'If you ask anything in My name, I will do it" (John 14:12-14).

The Bible has much to say about prayer, either directly or indirectly with respect to how it effects both a situation and the life of the one praying. To understand prayer, it is imperative to understand how the Bible views prayer. I think it's important that we understand that all expressions whether short or long crude or well-structured prayer, is in reality holding a conversation with God. How then shall I approach the King of Glory?

When we read Christ's promises regarding prayer we may jump to the conclusion that He has placed too much power into our hands – He says ask *"anything," "whatsoever," "what you will,"* and it shall be done. But He follows up with a qualifying phrase. He says we are to ask in His name.

That is the *one* condition – although it may be couched in different words the condition remains the same.

Therefore, if, we ask and do not receive, it can only be that we as not fulfilling the very clearly stated condition. Then truly being in Christ, we must prayerfully and carefully take great pains to discern just what it means to ask in His name; and we should not rest until we have fulfilled that condition.

THE PROMISE

Once again let us look at the promise: "Whatsoever you ask in My name, that will I do, that the Father may be glorified in the Son. If you ask anything in My name, I will do it" (John 14:13-14).

This is something new, in their hour of loss at Jesus' departure. He comforted them with the means that would provide them with the necessary resources to accomplish their task without His immediate presence which they had come to depend upon. We hear people more often then not in prayer, ask in Jesus' "name" as if it is an add-on to complete a formula at the end. God can not answer such prayers. In James 4:3, "We are told that those Christians were asking *"amiss."* We are to ask in Christ's name *"that the Father may be glorified in the Son"* (John 14:13).

In spite what is widely preached and taught today, we are not to seek wealth or health, prosperity or success, things and comfort, spirituality and fruitfulness in kingdom service simply for our own enjoyment, advancement or popularity, but only for Christ's sake – for His glory!

Just as a wrong prayer can't be made right by adding some mystical phrase; neither can a right prayer fail if some words are left out. Prayer is more than a question of words. Our Lord is interested in our faith and facts.

The chief goal of prayer is to glorify the Lord Jesus.

It is imperative that we know this – for it is the secret of all power in prayer. Jesus said, *"Many shall come in My name saying, 'I am Christ,' and shall deceive many"* (Matthew 24:5). He could have said as well, "And many shall *think* they are praying to the Father in My name, while deceiving themselves!" It means:

- The Christian's prayer should be for Christ's purposes and His kingdom not our selfish reasons.
- The Christian's prayer should be on the basis of Christ's merit and not any personal worthiness.
- The Christian's prayer should be in pursuit of Christ's glory only.

Five times over, our Lord repeats this simple condition, *"In My Name"* (see John 14:13, 14; 15:16; 15:16; 16:23, 24, 26). Without question we can see that this is very important to the Lord simply by the number of times He brought it up. It is more than a condition – it is also a promise, an encouragement, for our Lord's exhortations are always His enablements. A right understanding of the important words, "in My name" can be obtained through the following:

- There are some things that are done only for Christ's sakes, because of His atoning death. There is a subtle, very rapidly growing group within Christendom who do not believe in the atoning death of Christ, without a doubt these people cannot pray, "in His name." It is most important to remember the place and work of the shed blood of Jesus. For we are "justified by His blood" (see Romans 10:9, 10) and "we have "redemption through His blood, even the forgiveness of sins" (see Ephesians 1:7; Colossians 1:14). In response to a question raised by Thomas, Jesus declared, "I am the way, the truth, and the life, no one comes to the Father except through Me" (John 14:6). In this verse exclusiveness of Jesus as the only way to the Father is emphatic. Only *one way, not many ways, exist to God.* This is the sixth "I AM" statement of Jesus in John (see 6:35; 8:12; 10:7, 9; 10:11, 14; 11:25; 15:1, 5). Yes to pray "in the name of Jesus Christ" is to ask for things which the blood of Christ has secured ["purchased"] for us. We have "boldness to enter into the holiest, by the blood of Jesus" (Hebrews 10:19). There is no other way to the Father!

- The most familiar illustration of coming "in the name" of Jesus Christ is that of drawing money from a bank by means of a check. We can draw from our bank accounts *only* up to the amount of our deposit there. In my own by-name personal account I can go no further in making withdrawals. In the Bank of New York I have no money whatsoever, and therefore, I cannot withdraw any money from there. However, what if a very rich man who has a big account there gives me a blank check bearing his signature, and tells me to fill it out for any amount I choose, what shall I do? Should I just satisfy my present need, or shall I draw out as much as I can? I certainly don't want to offend my friend and benefactor, or lower myself in his high esteem of me. We hear much these days about heaven as our bank. God is the banker, "for every good gift and every perfect gift from above come down from the Father" (James 1:17). We need a "check" in order to make withdrawals from this limitless bank. *The Lord Jesus gives us a blank check in prayer.* He says, "Fill it in," for any amount; *ask 'anything' 'what you will,'* and you shall have it. Present your check in My name, and your request will be "honored." That's what happens when I go to the bank of heaven – when I go to the Lord in prayer. 1) I have nothing on deposit there; 2) I have absolutely no credit there; 3) therefore if I go in my own name I get absolutely nothing. But Jesus has unlimited credit in heaven, and He has granted me the privilege of going with His name on my checks; and when I go my prayers will be honored. To pray, then, in the name of Christ is to pray, not on the ground of my credit, but His. This is very true – not only for me, but all true children of God. Again, I say, "Jesus is the only way to God; therefore, ask only for those things that are according to His will – only for that which brings glory to His name. He also knows that if we truly love Him we won't ask for things He is not willing to give us. The bottom line here is that we cannot be sure that we are praying "in His name" unless we learn His will for us.

A BETTER WAY TO PRAY

When I go to Bank of Heaven in the name of our Lord Jesus Christ, with a check drawn on His unsearchable riches, God demands that I be worthy. I am definitely not worthy in the sense that I can merit or deserve anything from a holy God. But I am worthy in the sense that I am seeking the gift not for any glory of my own, but only for the glory of God.

Otherwise I can pray, but not receive anything. If our motives are not right – sooner or later we should realize that that's why we fail. The Scripture says, "You ask and receive not, because you ask amiss that you may spend it on your own pleasures" (James 4:3). Christ desires that we be so controlled by the Holy Spirit that we may *act* in Christ's name. Speaking of the Holy Spirit, He said,

"The Comforter …. Whom the Father will send in My name" (John 14:26).

"As many as are led by the Spirit of God, they are the sons of God" (Romans 8:14).

Jesus Christ said of Saul of Tarsus, "He is a chosen vessel unto Me to bear My name before the Gentiles and kings, and the children of Israel" (Acts 19:15).

So Paul says, "It pleased God to reveal His Son in Me." We cannot pray in Christ's name unless we bear His name before people. We can not do this except we "abide in Him" and His words abide in us. *Unless* the heart is right the prayer must be *wrong*.

Christ said, "If you abide in Me, and My words abide in you, you shall ask what you will, and it shall be done unto you" (John 15:7). These three promises are very similar and actually express the same thought in different words:

1. Ask anything in My name, I will do it (John 14:13, 14).
2. Ask what you will [if you abide in Me and My words abide in you], and it shall be done (John 15:7).
3. Ask anything, according to His will, we have the petitions (I John 5:14).

We can bring all of this together in the words of John, "Whatsoever we ask, we receive of Him, because we keep His commandments and do the things which are pleasing in His sight" (I John 3:22). When we obey His Word – He does what we ask! Listen to God and God will listen to you. God gives us a "power of attorney" over the kingdom of heaven – *if* only we fulfill the condition of abiding in Him.

It is only when whatever we do is done in Christ's name that He will do whatever we ask in His name.

We know that God's will is best for us. We know that He longs to bless us and make us a blessing. We know that to follow our own ideas is sure to hurt us and hurt also those we truly love. We should remember that "the secret of the Lord is with them that fear Him" (Psalm 25:14).

God's will is revealed in His Word in the Holy Scriptures. What He promises in His Word you and I can know it to be according to His will. For example, I may ask for wisdom, because His Word says, *"If any ....* *lack wisdom, let him ask of God .... And it shall be given him"* (James 1:5). We cannot be men and women of *prevailing prayer* unless we study God's Word to find out what His will is for us.

But the Holy Spirit of God is prayer's great Helper. Let's read again those beautiful words of the apostle Paul:

"In the same way the Spirit also helps us in our weakness; for we do not know what prayers to offer nor in what way to offer them, but the Spirit Himself pleads for us in yearnings that can find no words, and the Searcher of hearts knows what the Spirit's meaning is, because His intercessions for God's people are in harmony with God's will" (Romans 8:26, 27; Weymouth).

With such comforting words we are left without excuse. Is it not worthwhile to be whole-heartedly yielded to Christ? The half-hearted Christian is of no use to God or man. Hanging on to just one sin neutralizes our usefulness, our joy, and robs our prayer of its power!

Saints, we have caught a fresh glimpse of the grace and glory of our Lord and Savior, Jesus Christ. He is willing and waiting to share with us both His glory and His grace. He is willing to make us channels of blessings. Let us worship and serve God in sincerity and truth – eagerly crying and earnestly ask, "Lord what shall I do?" (Acts 22:10 RV). Then, in the power of His might – do it!

GOD'S DELAYS ARE NOT DENIALS

In this section we come to one of the most important questions that any person can ask. Much depends upon how each Christian answers. Does God always answer prayer? We would certainly agree that He does answer prayer – some prayers, and sometimes. Some so-called prayers He does not answer, simply because He does not hear them. When His people were rebellious, He said, *"When you make many prayers, I will not hear"* (Isaiah 1:15).

Certainly, every child of God should expect his or her prayers to be answered. The Apostle Paul declares, "All things are yours, for you are Christ's" (1 Corinthians 3:21). Yet, his wonderful declaration *seems* so plainly clear, but *very untrue* for most Christians. Yet it is definitely *not so*. They are ours! However, many Christians never come to possess their possessions.

I read an article about a farmer and his family who toiled day in and day out on their rocky acreage for years just barely surviving, never knowing that in the ground under their feet was one of the richest gold deposits the world has ever known. Here was tremendous wealth, yet unimagined and unrealized. It was "theirs," – yet it was not theirs!

If we really love the Lord, surely we would seek communion with Him in prayer more often? When our aim is solely the glory of God, then God can answer our prayers. Christ Himself rather than His gifts should be our desire.

"Delight yourself also in the LORD, trust in Him and He shall give you the desires of your heart" (Psalm 37:4).

Certainly, it is as true today as it was in the early church that men and women ask, and receive not, James says, *"Because you ask amiss, that you may spend it on your pleasures"* (James 4:3). He suggests that they were praying for the wrong things. Instead of praying for their own selfish desires, they should have been praying for God's will for them. But God is faithful that promised, and He will guard us from all evil and supply our every need; where there is a true loving relationship and in communion with the Lord and the brethren out of a clean heart, holy living and abiding faith in His finished work.

"Beloved if our heart does not condemn us, we have confidence toward God. And whatever we ask we receive from Him, because we keep His commandments and do those things that are pleasing in His sight" (1 John 3:21, 22).

The outworking of love

Jesus is the standard of love for all Christians. "A new commandment I give you, that you love one another." He says, "as I have loved you, that you love one another" (John 13:34). And He repeats: "This is My commandment that you love one another, as I have loved you" (15:12).

We are not to measure our Christian love against the love of some other Christian [and we usually pick someone whose life is far below the example] but against the love of Jesus Christ our Lord. If a Christian walks in the light and is in fellowship with God, he or she will also be in fellowship with others in God's family. It is easy to talk about Christian love, but much more difficult to practice it.

It is more than mere talk for a Christian to say that he or she loves the brethren, while he or she actually hates another brother or sister – therefore the person is really living a lie; and definitely out of God's will. Considering the two examples expressed in this section all of us should understand why our prayers are not answered.

It is impossible to be in fellowship with the Father and out of fellowship with another Christian at the same time.

This is one of the main reasons why God established the *local* church, the fellowship of believers. It has been said, "No man is an island." A person cannot live a complete and developing Christian life without fellowship with God's people. The contrast between those who are good at "saying," but takes no action in "doing"; and those who "say" and "do" grows wider and commitment dwindles as time passes in the local churches.

A pseudo religious-Christianity is overtaking many Christians individually and corporately. It is easy to practice a pseudo Christianity of "talking" of "singing the rights songs," of "using the right vocabulary," of "praying the right prayers" and through it all deceiving ourselves into *thinking* we are spiritual. Christian love that does not show itself in action and in attitude is **spurious** (see 1 Corinthians 13:4-7). The outworking of love when we are walking in the light? **"The seed of the Word"** can take root and bear fruit (see Luke 8:11).

CHAPTER 16 REVIEW: APPROACHING THE KING OF GLORY!

1. Discuss the "one" condition when asking "in Jesus' name."
2. List several reasons why we didn't receive what we asked for in prayer:
3. The chief goal of prayer is to glorify the Lord Jesus Christ.
4. Unless the heart is right, the prayer is wrong.
5. Discuss the outworking of love when we are walking in the light.

CHAPTER SEVENTEEN

ASK GOD AND TRUST HIM

"Beloved, if our heart does not condemn us, we have boldness toward God; and whatever we ask we receive of Him, because we keep His commandments, and do those things that are pleasing in His sight" (I John 3:21).

We *must* allow God to teach us that it is as natural for Him to answer prayer as it is for us to ask. He delights to hear our petitions, and certainly He loves to answer them! When we hear of some Hollywood star, professional athlete or some other wealthy person giving a great sum of money to relieve poverty in a certain area or to help fill a deficit in some other area of society, we exclaim, "How nice it would be if I could do something like that!" Well if we think about it God loves us – and we know that to be a true fact – don't you think it would give Him great joy and pleasure to give us what we ask?

I recall three answers to prayer out of many which Magdalene and I have witnessed over the years for greater boldness in coming to the Throne of Grace. While stationed in Panama during the early seventies, one afternoon after several days of a great Pentecostal camp meeting; traveling on the 56 mile trip by highway which crossed the country from

Panama City on the Pacific side back to Colon on the Atlantic side where we resided. As we crossed the interior of the country, we rounded a curve and on to a bridge about half way across we realized that we were right in the middle of a gunfight between Panamanian soldiers and rebels across the bridge; as I brought the car to a full stop to put the car in reverse my car stalled; which stopped the traffic behind me. With bullets flying my wife and I gathered our three small daughters and *walked* back to the entrance of the bridge. As we walked soldiers were advancing and rebels were retreating – we encountered both groups, but we walked pass them *safely* as if we were invisible.

After the battle moved away a couple came along and drove us back to our car which was totally untouched by either force. We got into the car, I turned the key, the engine started up and off we went on our way home singing, thanking and praising God for His abundant grace and mercy toward us.

On another occasion, one cold December morning I went out and warmed the car up for my wife to head out for school and her students a regular routine since I was now retired from the Army. We briefly kissed and just as she was about to shift into reverse two young men came running from behind a large bush in the yard. They forced us back into the house at gunpoint; the one guarding me noticed a portrait of me in uniform. He became furious cursing and taunting me to "just try something hero" and I'll blow you away." He told the other man to guard my wife in the front room, while he and I went through the house." He asked about guns in the house, I assured him that there were none.

He said as we went along I was to turn over the money and jewelry as we walked through each room of the house. He said he would search afterward and if he found one penny, a piece of jewelry or a gun, he would call out to his friend who would automatically blow my wife's brains out. It is a habit of mine to throw my silver change into a large jar and at some point I usually converted it to bills and paid car insurance or purchased gifts with it.

Once we reached my study, I showed him the jar with the change his eyes began to widen as he estimated the amount to be four or five hundred dollars. He called out to his friend to bring my wife into the office. Once my wife arrived, he snarled we don't leave any witnesses! My wife said, "We are just poor preachers …." That was all she was able to get out, as the man guarding her went into a nervous frenzy blurting out, "I told you we shouldn't stop here! The man guarding me was rattled by then; he picked up my check book and told me to make out a check for all the money in the account. I asked which one of them I should make the check out to. He just glared at me, threw the check book to the floor. After more cursing he forced us into the bathroom threatening what would happen if we didn't wait five minutes before we came out. Although they had the keys to the car which was still idling in the drive way – they were reported by witnesses to have left the house running. There are several footnotes to this miraculous deliverance from evil:

1. The door to my study was fully opened when we entered. After they were gone I went into my study to get some papers, as I turned to leave there it was in plain view a fully-loaded rifle that I had brought back from my father's house. I had totally forgotten all about it being there. What would have happened if he saw it? What might I have done if I had remembered the gun being there? My wife and I had prayed together [our daily devotion] just prior to our going out the door in the beginning; and we prayed throughout the ordeal and like the other incident and trusted God for the outcome – to God be the glory! The same two men hit another home after leaving us. As the wife got out of her car after working a shift overnight, the thieves made her ring the door bell, when her husband came to the door, the snarling fellow that was in our home earlier shot him point blank. The bullet somehow hit his spine and he has been in a wheelchair paralyzed from the waist down every since. This young man sat in his wheelchair very gracefully, patient and friendly throughout the entire trial. He took it all in stride and he was not bitter. Glory to God!

2. After years of doctor office visits and pills for diabetes II, three months ago my wife went to the doctor her blood-sugar was over 400. The doctor immediately wanted to send her for orientation on self-injections of insulin, which had been mentioned on prior visits. She refused and like Daniel and his three friends of the Old Testament, we prayed fervently for her total healing – restricting our diet of what the doctor had called all the "white stuff" [bread, rice, potatoes, and pasta, etc]. On June 15, 2017 she went to her scheduled appointment with the doctor. All of her

vital signs were normal, her blood-sugar was normal and she had lost ten pounds. All traces of diabetes were gone. Glory to God!

Stay prayed up!

My wife and I sometimes reminisce about going to church services and prayer meetings as youngsters, and though we were not in the same church; one point stood out among the older saints, they would admonish all to stay "prayed up!" This admonishment is very important in these what the apostle Paul called "perilous times" "the last days" (see II Timothy 3:1-17).

Evil lurks everywhere today. The national news media carried a story this past week approaching the 4th of July 2017 holiday. An irate motorist shot a young 18 year old girl in the head, killing her, as she was driving along [probably happily looking forward to college in the fall]. Whatever the cause of the rage, I'm sure that neither anticipated such an ending – two families in grief and turmoil. The nation witnesses on a daily basis "drive by shootings," "sexual assaults," involving innocent children as well as grown-ups, growing "home-grown" terrorism, "rising racial discard," a growing socio-economic divide coupled with a legal justice becoming the norm over moral justice.

Is there not a cause?

Certainly there is a cause all of us will agree if we would simply acknowledge these are perilous times, notice the biblical characterization of people in such a time:

- People will be lovers of themselves
- Lovers of money
- Boasters
- Proud
- Blasphemers
- Disobedient to parents
- Unthankful
- Unholy
- Unloving
- Unforgiving
- Slanderers

- Without self-control
- Brutal
- Despisers of good
- Traitors
- Headstrong
- Haughty
- Lovers of pleasure rather than lovers of God
- Having a form of godliness but denying its power

– Carefully study II Timothy 3:1-7

Perilous times and last days began at the writing of this letter and [*progresses*] until the return of Christ. A form of godliness [an outward appearance of reverence toward God]; that denies the power describes the greater part of religious activity. The great sin of the Pharisees was *hypocrisy* based on pride. Their religion was external, not internal; it was to impress people, not to please God:

- They bound people with heavy burdens – while Christ came to set people free (see Luke 4:18-19).
- They loved titles and public recognition and exalted themselves at the expense of others.
- They wore boxes containing portions of the Scriptures based on (Exodus 13:16; Deuteronomy 6:8; 11:18).
- They made the hems of their garments wide to advertise their religiosity (see Numbers 15:38).
- They had a form of godliness but no power to change lives (2 Timothy 3:5).
- The borders of Christ's garments gave forth power to change lives (Matthew 9:20; 14:36).
- For men to take the place of the father, or the Son of God, or the Holy Spirit is to disobey the Word of God and lead the people into error.

As time progresses people begin to participate in religious activities that are void of any connection or true relationship God or with individual *faith* in Jesus Christ. According to the Scriptures this kind of religion provokes God's anger. Matthew 23: 25-28 says,

"Woe to you, scribes and Pharisees, hypocrites! For you cleanse the outside of the cup and dish, but inside they are full of extortion and self-indulgence. Blind Pharisees, first cleanse the inside of the cup and dish, that the outside of them may be clean also.

"Woe to you, scribes and Pharisees, hypocrites! For you are like whitewashed tombs which indeed appear beautiful outwardly, but inside are full of dead men's bones and all uncleanness. Even so you also outwardly appear righteous to men, but inside you are full of hypocrisy and lawlessness.

Lessons from the Pharisees

The scribes and Pharisees were careful about tithing tiny seeds, but they failed to be obedient in more significant matters such as ensuring that all their actions were governed by justice, faith and mercy. Similarly we can become so preoccupied with external rules and regulations in the church that we forget the principles behind them. Christians individually and corporately can learn many lessons from the Pharisees.

The Pharisees formed as a group during the time in Israel's history when the nation was under intense pressure by the Greeks to give up their law and become liberal. The Scripture reflects men like Ezra remained true to the *faith*, protected the Law, and separated themselves from defilement (see Ezra 7:10). The time came when there were no prophets or teaching priests in Israel. Therefore the Pharisees "sat in Moses' seat." While Jesus Himself rejected many of the Pharisees teachings, He told the people to observe only those teachings that were true to the Law of Moses (see Matthew 5:21-6:18; 12:1).

The Pharisees having shunned God's righteousness were seeking to establish their own righteousness and teaching others to do so as well. Their legalism and self-righteousness effectively obscured the narrow gate by which the kingdom must be entered:

"Enter by the narrow gate; for wide is the gate and broad is the way that leads to destruction, and there are many who go in by it. Because narrow is the gate and difficult is the way which leads to life, and there are few who find it" (Matthew 7:13-14).

The tests of Righteousness (Matthew 7:13-29)

In the last section we saw that the Pharisees rejected God's righteousness and went about to establish their own unscriptural brand. Christ outlined three tests that will *prove* that our righteousness is truly from God and by it we can enter at the narrow gate. Pseudo Religious Christianity, a counterfeit, will always fail these tests:

A. The test of self denial (vv. 13-14). This is a test of two types of lifestyles: 1) The popular and comfortable life of ease and, 2) the difficult way of self-denial. One entered the narrow gate of surrender and the other the broad gate of self-sufficiency. True righteousness leads to self-denial. Demas failed the test (2 Timothy 4:10).

B. The test of spiritual fruit (vv. 15-23). In its makeup of "false prophets" is the fact that this includes false preachers who proclaim a false gospel, but primarily it speaks of false professors of *faith* in Christ. They parade around in sheep clothing, but inwardly their nature has not changed (see 2 Peter 1:4). They are unsaved though they call Jesus Lord and do outside religious deeds. How do we detect these false believers? Jesus said, *"You will know them by their fruit"* (v. 16). What fruit does Christ look for? He expects:

- The fruit of the Spirit [Christian character] as recorded in (Galatians 5: 22, 23).
- The fruit of the lips, testimony and praises to God (Hebrews 13:15).
- Holy living (Romans 6:22).
- Good works (Colossians 1:10).
- Souls won to Christ (Romans 1:13).

Professing Christians may be involved in religious activities, but they are not saved – however, those who are truly born again, *will reveal* these fruits in their daily living. Those professing but not possessing will be surprised at the judgment. We can fool ourselves. Satan blinds the mind and deceives people into *thinking* they are saved. Millions of professing Christians will be surprised to find out they were never saved at all!

C. The test of Obedience (Matthew 7:24-29). In this passage, the two builders represent two men in *this* life. They both use the same building materials and the same plans, and the world cannot tell the difference in their two houses. But when the storm comes *the time of testing* the house not founded on the rock crumbles and falls. <u>The true Christian is founded on the Rock, Christ Jesus</u> (1 Corinthians 3:11). Righteousness is not based on a denomination, a church, or a good life – but on Jesus Christ who died for the believer. A child of God is proven by obedience to Christ and standing through the storms of life that test him or her. Many have proved the reality of their faith by standing through the storms. True believers stand regardless of the test, because they were built on the Rock!

CHAPTER 17 REVIEW: TELL GOD AND THEN TRUST GOD

1. According to 1 John 3:21, whatever we ask of Christ, we receive of Him as we keep _____ _____ , and do those things that are pleasing to Him.
2. We can become so preoccupied with external rules and regulations in the church that we forget the principles behind them.
3. Contrast "hypocrisy" in the church with that of the Pharisees of old.
4. Discuss the three tests of righteousness.
5. Discuss legalism and self-righteousness and their affect on the church mission today.

CHAPTER EIGHTEEN

THE FRUIT OF GOD'S DIVINE PLAN

"But I do not want you to be ignorant, brethren concerning those who have fallen asleep, lest you sorrow as others who have no hope. For if we believe that Jesus died and rose again, even so God will bring with Him those who sleep in Jesus. For this we say to you by the word of the Lord, that we who are alive and remain until the coming of the Lord will by no means precede those who are asleep. For the Lord Himself will descend from heaven with a shout, with the voice of the archangel, and with the trumpet of God. And the dead in Christ will rise first. Then we who are alive and remain shall be caught up together with them in the clouds to meet the Lord in the air. And thus, we shall always be with the Lord. Therefore comfort one another with these words" (1 Thessalonians 4:13-18).

As I approach this chapter my mind goes back to my military days and the parades. As we moved onto the parade field, I would tell my soldiers this is it! Look alive now! As we make the last left turn and head down pass the reviewing stand the order rings out "eyes right!" As you "pass in review," your adrenalin is flowing, chest out, head high with a snappy hand salute – you hear the loud applause coming from the reviewing stand. You bore the sweltering sun in the heat of the day. It was well worth all that you went through to get here including fighting in the Vietnam War. You made it! It is your day of retirement. Through the years many have gone before you. You lived for this day!

WALK IN HOPE

In all of its excitement retirement day is nothing like Coronation day – when the true Church of God will meet Christ in the air [the Rapture]. In this classic passage on the rapture of the church, sorrow had come upon the saints in the church at Thessalonica concerning the death of their loved ones. They were concerned that in the rapture those who had already died would be left behind; never to be seen again, at the return of Christ for His church.

The rapture of the Church can happen at any moment – even today!

The apostle Paul assured them that their dead will be raised *first,* and that all the saints will be gathered together to meet Christ in the air. We are not to confuse the rapture of the saints with the revelation of the Lord, when He comes with His saints to earth to bring judgment and establish His kingdom. The Christian's race or warfare on this earth includes tension. The hope established in the promise of a future eternal rest in this passage helps the suffering Christians to endure present trials and tribulations (v. 4).

Presently the Lord is enthroned in glory at the right hand of the Father (John 17:5). The biblical record shows Christ standing to receive the spirit of His beloved saint, Stephen. He became the first Christian martyr (Acts 7:55, 56). After the death of Stephen, trials were common to the first century Christians. A careful study of the Book of Acts reveals that they were slandered, defamed, boycotted, mobbed, imprisoned, unemployed and many died for the faith.

Although so-called cultural progress may not have touched many of the cities in which Christians lived then, hostility toward the gospel and to Christians themselves was always present. Christians were targets of attacks because they no longer participated in pagan religious practices. Since they were the ones who abandoned the so-called gods of the people, Christians were blamed for everything from natural disasters to economic downturns.

With the news media mainly on the side of the cultural secular progressives most persecutions of Christians in the United States are suppressed. Those two factors mentioned above that caused persecution in the first century church are the same demonic-backed factors fueling much of the persecution we are seeing today:

1. Hatred for the gospel
2. Hostility toward Christians

Notice the similarity of cultural pressures on the first century church and the local churches of America today. However, unlike the early Christians who abandoned the gods of the people – the majority of the Christians today are seeking ways to assimilate the pagan gods and the practices of the culture, corporately and individually.

Many local churches are rewriting their by-laws and amending their constitutions to assimilate cultural values over biblical moral truth. Nationally speaking, it is appalling to see the rejection of the name of Jesus in the public square and marketplace, seeing other faiths given priority over Christianity to the point of entering prison and hospital chapels void of the cross. The cross is the symbol of our faith, yet we hide it away in some closet in fear of offending the *religion* of any non-Christian groups; all simply because the culture has deemed all religious faiths equal. God forbid!

SUFFERING FOR GOD'S GLORY

The apostle Peter admonished Christians, *"Do not think it strange concerning the fiery trial which is to try you, as though some strange thing happened to you; but **rejoice** to the extent that you partake of Christ's sufferings, that when His glory is revealed you may also be glad with exceeding joy. If you are reproached for the name of Christ, blessed are you, for the Spirit of glory and of God rests upon you. On the other part He is blasphemed, but on your part He is glorified"* (1 Peter 4:12-14).

When Christians suffer unjustly on behalf of Christ, they discover that the close relationship they have with God during that period will refresh their spirit. For Christians the purpose of suffering is to:

- *prove* their true character
- clear away the dross of sin
- allow the pure nature of Christ to demonstrate itself
- expect suffering and prepare for it
- for the glory of God

Without a doubt suffering will be a part of the Christian experience until Christ returns (see Romans 8:18-22).

Judgment at the House of God

"The time has come for judgment to begin at the house of God; and if it begins with us first, what will be the end of those who do not obey the gospel of God?" (1 Peter 4:17).

Now *"If the righteous one is scarcely saved, where will the ungodly and the sinner appear"* (v. 18).

The focus of these verses is not on a building, but on believers, and also "those who do not obey." Peter speaks of those who are not part of God's eternal family as being disobedient (2:7, 8; 3:1, 20).

Judgment does not always mean condemnation in Scripture. When used in conjunction to Christians, it consistently refers to evaluation of a believer's works for the purpose of rewards:

"According to the grace of God which was given to me, as a wise master builder I have laid the foundation, and another builds on it. But let each one take heed how he builds on it. For no other foundation can anyone lay than that which is laid, which is Jesus Christ. Now if anyone builds on this foundation with gold, silver, precious stones, wood, hay, straw, each one's work will become will become clear: for the Day will declare it, because it will be revealed by fire; and the fire will test each one's work, of what sort it is. If anyone's work is burned, he will suffer loss, but he himself will be saved, yet so as through fire" (1 Corinthians 3:10-15).

Paul established the church of Corinth on the foundation of Christ, *gold, silver, precious stone, wood, hay, straw:* These building materials refer to:

- the quality of work by the Corinthians
- their motivations
- the kind of doctrine they taught

The **Day** in verse 13 speaks of the time when Christ will judge the merit of each of His servants' work and reward them accordingly:

*"For we must all appear before the judgment seat of Christ, that **each one** may receive the things done in the body, according to what he [or she] has done, whether good or bad. Knowing therefore, **the terror of the Lord,** we persuade men; but we are well known with God, and I also trust are well known in your conscience"* (2 Corinthians 5:10-11). Bracket mine.

Our wanting to be with Jesus produces an ambition within us to please Him in all that we do in this life. The person who is *unconcerned* about doing good deeds show very little vision. The terror of the Lord *is* the fear of standing before the Lord and having one's life exposed and evaluated. Christians must all appear before the judgment seat of Christ. Sinners will not appear at this judgment.

THE THRONES AND JUDGMENTS

Whether good or bad we will all stand in judgment, therefore it is extremely important that we briefly cover the judgments. Many sincere believers are thoroughly misled into thinking there will be a "general" judgment. Neither a general judgment nor general resurrection is taught in the Word of God. The Scripture clearly speaks of *five* separate judgments and *three* thrones:

The Three Thrones

1. *The judgment seat of Christ* – mentioned in II Corinthians 5:10. This will take place in the air just after the Rapture and it will be for *believers* only.

2. *The throne of His glory* – described in Matthew 25:31, 32. This will be here on the earth. It is the judgment of the nations.
3. *The Great White Throne* – as set forth in Revelation 20:11-15. This will be in heaven and only *the wicked* will be judged there.

The Five Judgments

1. *Judgment Number One*

This judgment concerns "sin" which Jesus judged when He died on the cross. When a person believes on Jesus and puts his or her trust in His finished work, that person is redeemed. God does not want His children to sin. He does not give us permission to sin; but He has made provision for us if we stumble and fall (see I John 2:1; I John 1:9).

2. *Judgment Number Two*

This judgment will be believers before the "Judgment Seat of Christ" and having to do with their "stewardship and works." No sinners will be judged here for sin is not in question here. The result is the "receiving of rewards or the loss of rewards" "but he himself [or herself] shall be saved" (see Corinthians 3:11-15).

Yes, a believer can lose his or her reward; but *Jesus Christ is our salvation.* When by faith we place our hand in His precious nail-scarred hand, He is able to keep us through His mighty power. We are warned to hold fast that which we have, that we don't lose our *crown* – but certainly a crown is not our salvation.

There are *five* crowns mentioned in the New Testament which can be earned by a believer through faithful stewardship:

1. The incorruptible crown (I Corinthians 9:25).
2. The crown of rejoicing (I Thessalonians 2:19).
3. The crown of righteousness (II Timothy 4:8).
4. The crown of life (James 1:12).
5. The crown of glory (1 Peter 5:4).

If you study carefully each of these Scriptures, you will know the clearly stated requirements for coming into possession of one [or all five] of these crowns. Again, some believers will receive a full reward. Others will lose their reward, and their works will be burned up.

The great danger for believers today is unfaithfulness to the true gospel of grace.

---

3. Judgment Number Three

The subject of this judgment will be the Jews during the Tribulation period. The basis of this judgment will be the Jew's rejection of Jesus. The results will be finally the conversion of the Jews and their acceptance of Jesus as their Messiah. The basis of the judgment of the Jews is their rejection of the Godhead. In the days of Samuel they rejected God the *Father* (1 Samuel 8:7). In the days of Jesus they rejected God the *Son* (Luke 23:18). In the early days of Christianity, the days of the infant Church, they rejected God the *Holy Spirit* (Acts 7:51, 54-60). For their sin, the Jews have been scattered to the ends of the earth, into every nation under the sun. This will continue to haunt them until the end of the "time of the Gentiles" be fulfilled. When the time of the Gentiles are about to end, the Jews will return to the land of Israel [returning there as unbelievers]. The Man of Sin, Antichrist will be revealed. It will be the bloodiest time this earth will ever know, and during that time the seven vials of the wrath of God will be poured out upon this earth (see Revelation 15:1, 5-8; 16:1-21). The Jews will cry out to God for mercy:

"And I will pour upon the house of David, and upon the inhabitants of Jerusalem, the Spirit of grace and of supplications: and they shall look upon me whom they have pierced, and they shall mourn for Him, as one mourns for his only son, and shall be in bitterness for Him, as one that is in bitterness for his firstborn" (Zechariah 12:10). It is at this time that Christ will appear on the Mount of Olives (Zechariah 14:3, 4).

The Jews will look upon Him *"whom they have pierced"* and a nation will be born (converted) in a day: "Who has heard such a thing? Who has seen such things? Shall the earth be made to bring forth in one day? Or shall a nation be born at once? As soon as Zion travailed, "she brought forth her children" (Isaiah 66:8).

This will complete the judgment of the Jews. They will be ushered into the kingdom.

4. Judgment Number Four

The subjects of this judgment will be the Gentile nations. The time of this judgment will be the revelation of Christ when He comes with ten thousand of His saints. The judgment will take place at the throne of His glory in the valley of Megiddo. The judgment will be based on the treatment extended by the Gentile nations toward the Jews during the tribulation period. This will result in some nations being saved and other nations will be destroyed (see Matthew 25:31-46). Therefore at this judgment Christ will say to the "sheep" nations, "Come you blessed of My Father, inherit the kingdom prepared for you from the foundation of the world .... in as much as you have done this unto one of the least of these My brethren (the Jews), you have done it unto Me" (see Matthew 25:34, 40). The sentence for the "goat" nations will be:

"Depart from Me, you cursed, into everlasting fire, prepared for the devil and his angels.

And they shall go away into everlasting punishment ...." (see Matthew 25:41, 46).

5. Judgment Number Five

The subject of this judgment will be the wicked dead based on the works of the wicked, and the results this judgment will be that the wicked will be cast eternally into the lake of fire. This judgment is found in Revelation 20:11-15:

*"And I saw a great white throne, and He that sat on it, from whose face the earth and the heaven fled away; and there was found no place for them. And I saw the dead, small and great, stand before God; and the books were opened: and another book was opened, which is the **book of life:** and the dead were judged out of the things which were written in the books, according*

to their works. *"And the sea gave up the dead which were in it; and death and hell delivered up the dead which were in them: and they were judged every man according to their works. And death and hell were cast into the lake of fire. This is the second death. <u>And whosoever was not found written in the book of life was cast into the lake of fire.</u>"*

At the Great White Throne judgment the unsaved will not be judged as to whether they are saved or lost. They will be judged to ascertain the degree of their punishment in the Lake of Fire.

Some will be sentenced to more severe punishment than others, but none will escape punishment.

Yes, sinner and saint will be judged – but not at the same judgment. Believers will be judged at the Marriage Supper of the Lamb immediately following the Rapture. The unsaved will be judged at the end of time, just before eternity begins.

CHAPTER 18 REVIEW: THE FRUIT OF GOD'S DIVINE PLAN

1. Suffering will be a part of the Christian experience until Christ returns. Discuss reasons for suffering on page 196.
2. Discuss the Day in I Corinthians 3:13 which speak of the time when Christ will judge the merit of each of His servants. Review page 197.
3. All Christians must stand before judgment seat of Christ.
4. Carefully review and discuss the three thrones on page 198.
5. Review and discuss the five judgments on page 198.

CHAPTER NINETEEN

THE MINISTRY OF RECONCILIATION

"Now all things are of God, who has reconciled us to Himself through Jesus Christ, and has given us the ministry of reconciliation" (II Corinthians 5:18).

In Psalm 34:8 we are invited to *"taste and see that the Lord is good."* This is an invitation to you and me to *experience* God for ourselves. Second Corinthians 3:18 tells us that in some wonderful way, we can behold the Lord's glory.

As wonderful as words are for describing and talking about God, nothing, I repeat nothing can compare to actually *experiencing* Him, seeing Him, hearing His voice, or feeling His presence.

When Jesus walked the earth two thousand years ago, the apostle John could truthfully write that he had seen, heard, and touched the Word of life (1 John 1:1-3). God intends for us to experience His presence in a unique and powerful way through His Spirit and His Word working in tandem.

In II Corinthians 3:18, *"We all"* is a line of demarcation in this passage. Paul is speaking of "all" truly born again Christians in contrast to unbelievers.

For example, when an unbeliever reads the Bible he or she finds it dull and full of hidden meaning. But when a believer reads the Bible he or she reads the *living words* – and sees Jesus as:

- "a root out of dry ground"
- "the Rose of Sharon"
- "the Lily of the Valley"
- "the Bright and Morning Star"
- "One altogether lovely, pure, holy, glorious, and mighty"

Ask a sinner, "What do you think of Christ?" and you will get a variety of answers. Ask a true believer, "What do you think of Christ?" and he or she will declare that Christ is my Savior, my Friend, the One in whom I put my hope, the One who will receive me into heaven when this life is over.

RECONCILIATION THROUGH A NEW CREATION

*"Therefore if any man be in Christ, he is a **new creature [creation]**; old things are passed away behold, all things are become new"* (1 Cor. 5:17).

There is no "maybe" about it – a man or woman, boy or girl in Christ is a new creature….." As was stated in an earlier chapter all truly born again believers are "in Christ." Apart from being in Christ – there is *absolutely* no hope for any human being. Let no smooth-talking false teacher, or pseudo-religious Christian tell you anything different. In Colossians 1:20-29 the apostle Paul explained,

"It pleased the Father that in Him all the fullness should dwell, and by Him to reconcile all things to Himself, by Him, whether things on earth or things in heaven, having made peace through the blood of His cross. And you who once were alienated and enemies in your mind by wicked works, yet now He has reconciled in the body of His flesh through death, to present you holy, and blameless, and above reproach in His sight – if indeed you continue in the faith, grounded and steadfast, and are not moved away from the hope of the gospel which was preached to every creature under heaven, of which I, Paul, became a minister. I now rejoice in my sufferings for you, and fill up in my flesh what is lacking in the afflictions of Christ, for the sake of His

body, which is the church, of which I became a minister according to the stewardship from God which was given to me for you, to fulfill the word of God, the mystery which has been hidden from ages and from generations, but now has been revealed to His saints. To them God willed to make known what are the riches of the glory of this mystery among the Gentiles: which is Christ in you the hope of glory. Him we preach, warning every man and teaching every man in all wisdom, that we may present every man perfect in Christ Jesus. To this end I also labor, striving according to His working which works in me mightily."

All over the world people are seeking peace. They are seeking peace with members of their family, friends, neighbors, co-workers, supervisors, governments and among races of people. A few trips around the mountain will more than prove to us that a manmade solution to peace only gives temporary or surface relief. Finding peace with God is the only solution to anyone's quest for peace. Paul says, "Peace only comes through reconciliation." He wants them to remember how wonderful reconciliation really is. God had done a marvelous thing for them.

Reconciliation through Christ

It is imperative that all humanity knows that the secret to peace and reconciliation with God is the cross of Christ. God loves His Son so much that He will accept anyone who honors His Son through authentic trust and belief. If a person believes that his or her sins are forgiven through the cross of Christ, Then God will forgive their sins. Therefore if an individual believes that the blood of Jesus reconciles them to God. God will reconcile that individual.

He will allow the person with true faith to draw near Him. The great passage of Scripture above is one of the great studies on the message of reconciliation. What does it mean to reconcile? It means to restore relationships, harmony and communion with God.

Men and women, boys and girls can now be reconciled to God; meaning they can be restored to and accepted by God, because of Christ's work on Calvary. People must now turn to God through faith in the blood of Christ. This passage carries astronomical importance because it also reveals that along with people God has reconciled the whole universe to Himself whether they are things in the earth or things in heaven. God has done all He can:

- He has made it possible for people to draw near to Him through reconciliation.
- It is a person's choice to draw near to Him through reconciliation.
- God has done His part. "It is finished!"

GOD'S ONE GREAT PURPOSE IN RECONCILIATION

*"But the day of the Lord will come as a thief in the night; in which the heavens will pass away with a great noise, and the elements will melt with fervent heat; both the earth and the works that are in it will be burned up. Therefore, since all these things will be dissolved, **what manner of persons ought you to be** in holy conduct and godliness, looking for and hastening the coming of the day of God, because of which the heavens will be dissolved, being on fire, and the elements will melt with fervent heat? Nevertheless we according to His promise, look for a new heaven in which righteousness dwell"* (2 Peter 3:10-13).

The Day of the Lord will have a surprise arrival, sudden, unexpected, and disastrous to the unprepared. In I Thessalonians 5:2, Paul says, "For you yourselves know perfectly that the day of the Lord so comes as a thief in the night. For when they say, "Peace and safety!" then suddenly destruction comes upon them, as labor pains upon a pregnant woman. And they shall not escape."

The idea in the verses is to look ahead to the life that will exist in the new heaven and new earth. The life of the future will be a *life of reconciliation* with God, a life that will see everything in the new heavens and earth reconciled to God. This does not mean that murderers, adulterers, idolaters, and a host of other unbelievers will be there. It means that everyone who is there will be reconciled to God. Emphasis added.

Living in Unparalleled Times

We are living in unparalleled times. Is the world getting better or worse? I think the proper answer to that question would depend on the lenses through which a person is viewing it, from biblical or cultural lenses. Surveying the three Synoptic Gospels, Matthew, Mark, and Luke, then narrowing the lenses to Jesus' Parable of the Sower – we would have to agree with Jesus' observation that the bad is growing worse as days go by [the media keeps us abreast of that], but the good is getting better [individuals are giving more, and community enablement programs and volunteerism are on the rise, [just to name a few]. We are living increasingly in "the best of times and the worse of times" (Dickens):

- Good and evil
- Beauty and ugliness
- Life and death

Each flourishes right next to the other neither good nor evil seem to be getting the upper hand. How about your church? I think that the means have become the ends in many of the local churches. Some pew research, that there are *over* 80 million Americans in the pews of churches every Sunday. That's more than the entire attendance of every professional football, basketball, baseball, and hockey arena *combined* – for *an entire year!*

Yet sadly, this massive number of churchgoers is almost irrelevant to the culture. How is it that the riches churches in the world are making their smallest impact on society than at any time ever before in history? Think about that! How can it be so? Of that great number of churchgoers above what percentage is really authentic born again Christians? In this country, we are big on numbers even in the local churches. So with these churches, their attendance statistics is the proof in the pudding for them; sadly for many a true salvation experience is not a priority. In fact many churches are receiving the unsaved into their membership hoping that the salvation experience will eventually happen, mainly through association? In the early Church when a Jew was converted, as Paul was:

- He or she no longer looked down on Gentiles or hated Christians.
- His prejudices toward Christianity were gone.
- His attachments to the rites, ceremonies, holy days, and holidays [things that he had depended on for salvation] were gone forever.
- He no longer believed that only Jews were supposed to be saved.
- He received all brethren who are in the faith [Jude 3]; he believed they all belong to the family of God.

By the same token, when a Gentile was converted and became a true believer:

- Idols were done away with.
- Love for sin and ungodliness passed away.
- Old habits and practices, old prejudices, opinions, and attachments – pass away, and the love of God and the Holy Spirit fills the vacancy (see Romans 5:5).
- There is such a deep, radical change that takes place when a person is truly born again – *that the change can easily be seen and recognized by unbelievers.*
- The *understanding* of a believer changes. Praise God! When one is an unbeliever he or she may say, "I cannot *understand* the Bible." But when that sinner is born again he or she recognizes that while they may not *understand* all of God's Word, he or she does understand many passages that were formerly blocked out or closed to his or her unregenerate mind.
- Thus as the convert studies and walks in the light of God's Word, their *understanding* becomes clearer.
- He or she changes their mind about God and the things of God.
- Through the Spirit and the Word working in tandem, the convert is transformed as their mind is renewed (Romans 12:1-5).
- Old thoughts pass away and new thoughts about God take over.
- Other Christians become your new friends, and there is a new beauty about everything that was ugly and unattractive.
- The believer sees the universe with new eyes because he or she has a new heart.
- The convert experiences a new love for family and friends.
- New feelings rise in the heart for all men.

All things come of you, O Lord

*"Now **all things are of God** who has reconciled us to Himself through Jesus Christ, and has given us **the ministry of reconciliation,** that is, that God was in Christ reconciling the world to Himself, not imputing their trespasses to them, and has committed to us **the word of reconciliation"** (2 Corinthians 5:18-19). Emphasis added.*

Folks this is so much more than much of this generation can process when considering what they have or better said have not been taught in their homes and local churches. In chapter sixteen, I covered the judgments so that you can understand the importance of your personal trust and dependence on God. Remember every Christian will stand before God as our works will be tested (see Romans 14:10).

We do not work to be saved, but we work because we are saved. We want to please God. Don't you want hear Him say to you, "Well done!" Because God has given us all these things – the renewed heart, the renewed mind and all things new [a new creation].

Reconciliation is God's work of Love, a work carried out by Jesus Christ. He came to reveal God's nature and God's love toward humankind even though man had wickedly sinned. Christ came to accomplish the work of reconciliation and to purchase our redemption by taking a body like our body except it was sinless. In that body He lived a pure, sinless life, and by means of His death for our sins and His bodily resurrection for our justification, and by sending the Holy Spirit to work His blessed will in us. The Holy Spirit humbles and convicts the individual of sin and when he or she hears the Word of God and receives it, the Holy Spirit miraculously quickens the human spirit to new birth from above.

The Ministry of Reconciliation

God has given those who are genuinely His, the glorious privilege and opportunity to make known to others the nature and plan of reconciliation. Every truly born again Christian then, is commissioned by the Lord Jesus Christ to make known this glorious *truth*. We are to carry the message of salvation to people everywhere, especially our areas of influence: family, friends, neighbors, and marketplace; urging them to accept God's love and His plan of redemption. The essence of our message is "God was in Christ reconciling the world to Himself." Jesus said, **"I am in the Father and My Father in Me"** (John 14:10). Emphasis added throughout.

In a study of John 17, you will see the *Oneness* of God the Father and God the Son. It pleased God that *in Christ* should all the fullness dwell, and **"in Christ"** the true believer is complete (see Colossians 2:9-10). When one believes and is redeemed, God regards that believer's sin as though it had never happened.

This is the covenant that I will make them, after those days, said the Lord: *"I will put My laws into their hearts, and in their minds, will I write them; and their sins and iniquities will I remember no more"* (Hebrews 10:16, 17). Emphasis added.

God's divine purpose and plan embraces all humanity – the whole world. "For God so loved the world ...." (John 3:16). Christ is the propitiation for *"the sins of the whole world"* (I John 2:2).

In Romans 3:24-26 Paul explains it this way, *"being justified freely by His grace through the redemption that is in Christ Jesus, whom God set forth as a propitiation by His blood through faith, to demonstrate His righteousness, because in His forbearance God has passed over the sins that were previously committed, to demonstrate at the present time His righteousness, that He might be just and the justifier of the one who has faith in Jesus."*

The apostle Paul has shown that men could not be regarded righteous on any merit of their own, or by personal obedience to the Law. He now affirms that if they are so treated as righteous it has to be *by unmerited favor, "by His grace."* We hear much preaching today in the name of "fresh grace" "modern grace" and even of a "grace revolution." Many are led to believe that grace is "their right" but it is "freely" given – a gift. This is what the gospel is all about.

There is no distinction – all must be redeemed alike, through the redemption that is "in Christ Jesus." Looking back in summary of vv. 24-26, we see the Gospel which means "good news" of salvation. From this we get a seven-point Word of Reconciliation:

The Word of Reconciliation

1. Salvation is free (v. 24). Salvation is without cost and without price. The sinner is justified [or pronounced righteous] by God when he or she *receives* Jesus as Savior – who paid the price (see John 1:12, 13).

2. Salvation is by and through grace – the unmerited favor of God (v. 24). There is absolutely nothing a sinner can do or give to merit salvation.

3. Salvation is by and through the redemptive work of the Lord Jesus Christ ....through the redemption that is in Christ Jesus: whom God has set forth to be propitiation ...." (vv. 24-25). "Redemption" means to "buy back." Jesus bought us back at the tremendous price of His shed blood. All humanity belongs to God, our Creator. Satan has never created a human being; however, only those who are saved belong to Christ by redemption. Jesus bought back all that the devil stole from Adam and Eve. During the days of the tabernacle on the great day of atonement, when the high priest *sprinkled* the sacrificial blood on the golden top of the ark (see Leviticus 16:14), it became a place of *mercy* and ceased to be a place of *judgment*. Thus, our Lord and Savior, Jesus Christ is both the Mercy Seat and the Sacrifice (the propitiation), whereby mercy is offered to a sinner by faith.

4. Salvation is for those who believe *"through faith"* (v.25). Only believers have salvation. You can belong to a church and not be saved. You can embrace and follow a religion and not be saved. Those who are saved received their salvation through faith. *"Believe on the Lord Jesus Christ, and you shall be saved"* (Acts 16:31).

5. Salvation is based upon the shedding of blood and *"through faith in His blood"* (v. 25). It was by the blood of atonement on the mercy seat – the offering of a bullock on the Great Day of Atonement that reconciliation was concluded in the Old Testament era. Our salvation is also by blood atonement – but it is His (Christ's) own blood. Many theologians have publically denied the virgin birth, His blood atonement, and the bodily resurrection of our Lord. But please know, *without the shedding of blood there is no remission of sin* (Hebrews 9:22). No person will ever get to heaven unless he or she is covered by the blood of Jesus.

6. Salvation is retrospective in its effect: *".... to declare His righteousness for the remission of sins that are past ...."*(v. 25) or "to show His righteousness because of the passing over of sins done before the cross – but the sin-debt had to be paid. Jesus died for the sins of Adam just as much as for our sins. The blood Christ

shed on Calvary covered all of the Old Testament era offerings and even back to the covering God put on Adam and Eve in the Garden.

7. Salvation is also seen in its effect: *"that He might be just and the justifier of him who believes in Jesus"* (v. 26). The cross took care of all the sins of the Old Testament era – and declares a believing sinner in this New Testament era of grace saved by the mercy and righteousness of God for his or her salvation rests on the fact that their sins have been paid for and justice maintained. Thus God is just and at the same time the Justifier of all believing sinners.

In summary, the ministry of reconciliation speaks to the reality that God wills sinful men to be reconciled to Himself (see Romans 5:10; Ephesians 4:17-24). God also gave us a word of reconciliation – in the section above we see that Paul gave us a true and trustworthy word; which opposes the false and unsure one that fills the world today. Truth counters that false message.

Because all humanity existed in the loins of Adam, and have through procreation inherited his depravity, it can be said that all sinned in him. Therefore, humans are not sinners because they sin – but rather they sin because they are sinners.

AMBASSADORS FOR CHRIST

*"Now then, we are ambassadors for Christ, as though God were pleading **through us**: we implore you on Christ's behalf, **be reconciled to God"** (II Corinthians 5:20).

We are ambassadors for Christ. This applies to all believers; although it is true God calls and appoints some of us to give our lives in special full-time ministry making known the good news of salvation. However as stated earlier all believers are ambassadors in the spiritual sense. I said, we are all called to make God's message of His glorious saving grace known to the world.

An ambassador is sent in the interest of their own country, and such an ambassador is under obligation to obey the instructions of his or her sovereign. A footnote from my own experience, concerning embassy duty, all needs are provided for the Ambassador and staff by the government that sent them. The ambassador does not have to rely on the host country for anything.

As Christ's ambassadors all of our needs are met and supplied by God, who sent us. We are to do what Christ would do if He were here in person. We are to make known the gospel of salvation and declare the whole truth of God's love and reconciliation. Just as the ambassadors of national leaders such as kings and presidents have no right to negotiate or change the terms laid down by the one who sent them – so the ambassadors of Christ have no right to follow their own desires or plans. We must obey the instructions of our Sovereign, Jesus Christ, or suffer the consequences of our rejection and disobedience. To be an ambassador for the Lord is a high calling which carries a very serious responsibility.

The message of the man or woman of God is to be regarded as the message of God – because God's ambassadors deliver the Word of God. The message entrusted to us reemphasizes that *all believers* have something to do in God's redemptive plan:

- This speaks to the reality that God wills that sinful man be reconciled unto Himself (carefully study Romans 5:10; Ephesians 4:17-24).

- God has called all believers to proclaim the gospel of reconciliation to others, with the intention that they do the same (1 Corinthians 1:17).

- God wants all Christians to accept the privilege of serving unbelievers by proclaiming a desire to be reconciled.

- God created humankind for His glory, praise and honor.

God was in Christ

God was: "in Christ" is two words that comprise a brief but most profound statement of the inexhaustible significance of the believer's redemption. In His great love and mercy God has done all He can do to help humanity escape the damnation of an eternal hell. He gave His only begotten Son to pay the sin-debt of humankind by His suffering and death on the cross.

Jesus paid the sin-debt for the whole world, and in Him God is satisfied:

1. **God** loved sinners so much that He has removed all obstacles to reconciliation between Himself and humankind. He has done all that is *needful* to bring about reconciliation between a just and holy God and a sinner.

2. **Jesus** loved sinners so much that He willingly left His father's bosom and came to the womb of the Virgin Mary to be born in a body of humiliation in order that He could, and did *die* for sinners.

3. **The Holy Spirit** loves sinners so much that He came into the world on the Day of Pentecost and never left. He is convicting and winning people through true pastors, evangelists, teachers and other caring Christians through the *power* of the gospel to "be reconciled to God!"

REVIVE US AGAIN

How much do **we** love sinners? While many Christians claim that they would love to experience revival in their church, community or town, most are convinced that nothing will happen. But revival is one the ways God energizes a church, community, town, even a *whole country*. God has tied revival to an outpouring of the Holy Spirit; therefore the fact that many of the reasons people believe their church can never experience revival – could be the very signal that God is going to do some thing very special in their midst.

Sadly the outpouring of the Holy Spirit in 1906 Los Angeles revival has been largely ignored for nearly a century. While the Holy Spirit is a person, on occasion the Scriptures portray Him as being "poured out" like water on thirsty people in need of the blessings of God. The out pouring marks a period of time that the spiritual intensity of the Holy Spirit's presence is recognized by others and a breakout of revival is experienced by Christians. Historically, the unsaved are awakened to their need for salvation and society is eventually reformed.

Revival can come to any church if the people are prepared to meet the conditions God has required. Most of our local churches believe in the importance of evangelism, but few consistently practice it. William P. Mackay

---

Evangelism involves communicating the gospel in the power of the Holy Spirit to unconverted people with the sole intent of effecting conversions.

When our local churches institute an evangelistic ministry those persons who repent of their sin and trust Christ for salvation are encouraged to join and serve the Lord as part of the local church. Churches that are truly biblically engaged concern themselves with training and *producing* 2 Timothy 2 believers who in turn reach others for Christ.

Revival's message

Some things in church are timeless, unchanging, and *nonnegotiable precepts* that are based on Scripture and are *mandates for all churches* to pursue to accomplish their purpose. Like the apostle Paul for instance, we must not be ashamed of the gospel, for it is the *power* of God unto salvation. Many churches have lost the gospel of salvation due to biblical illiteracy, misappropriation of privilege, choosing the opportunity to raise funds or just entertainment purposes. The same Holy Spirit who empowers us for effective evangelism also empowers the Scriptures to be effective in saving souls (see 2 Timothy 3:15). Emphasis added.

The Scripture is referred to as the "Word of life" because the Bible is the Word of God that produces spiritual life (see Philippians 2:16). It is much easier to effectively witness after you have committed Scripture to memory, knowing that you are carrying the Word of spiritual life to others. A desire to tell others about Jesus becomes natural for you.

Revival fails in many efforts because the gospel [the power] is not activated through preaching – which is the proper tool for getting the job done. Then there is the tendency toward self-centeredness which was in the church from the beginning. When Jesus told the disciples to wait in

Jerusalem until the Holy Spirit had come upon them; they wanted to know, "Lord, is it at this time you are restoring the kingdom to Israel?" (Acts1:6). Like many local churches today the disciples probably thought this meant that the whole world would come to Jerusalem and to them in particular! However, His *mandate* for His disciples is instead for them to go to the world.

The Church is found in buildings, mainly on Sundays; but it does not belong there. The Church belongs outside – and that goes for the church, everywhere!

The message of the gospel is to be preached to every available person in the whole world, by every available means. Paul summarized the message of the gospel when he wrote,

"Christ died for our sins, according to the Scriptures, and he was buried, and that he rose again the third day according to the Scriptures" (1 Corinthians 15:3-4).

When the whole Christian community begins to adhere to and practice this – their message will consistently point people to the Savior. God did not give all of His gifts to one individual or one denomination or one congregation in the city, but He distributed them all over the body of Christ to build up the body. Though believers come from various Christian communities that are culturally and theologically distant from each other; it must be remembered that such distance is man-made. Unbelievers loved to hang out with Jesus, because there was different about Him that drew other people to Him. People in our area of influence family, neighbors, and people in the workplace should feel the same way about us, as we reflect His glory on earth (see Luke 10:16).

One of the outstanding traits of Christ toward all people was His kindness. He fellowshipped with them over dinner, showing them His unconditional acceptance of them just the way they were. We often fail in this area many times showing our disdain for those who are classified as sinners to the max. This destructive attitude is unworthy of Christ and His kingdom.

Showing an authentic loving and caring attitude toward the person is in order prior to proclamation; let's the individual know that you are with them; offer prayer if in a moment of crisis. Unbelievers know that God has a solution, but many times because of guilt and unbelief they are afraid to pray.

If you are willing to pray then on their behalf, they will be most thankful for it, regardless of how things work out. I say pray *then,* because they have little respect for our promise to pray for them later. The peace incurred because of our honest concern in prayer is what the unbeliever lacks the most. Therefore, you have provided them with the most protective and healing fellowship possible. Certainly you have gained a friend and improve the spiritual climate in your relationship.

As I stated in an earlier section, the church was born on the streets of Jerusalem, but the most powerful and dramatic power demonstrations recorded in the Book of Acts happened in other locations after they had left Jerusalem; thus, we have the wisdom and *mandate* of going to the lost rather than waiting for them to come in to us (see Acts 8-12).

God's strategic plan is for the body to grow together. Try to imagine walking into the lobby of a hotel and there lying right in your path is an unattached arm, what would be your reaction? One thing you would know for sure; the arm is dead, because it can't possibly live unattached from the body.

The lack of spiritual and biblical teaching and training even for many manning the pulpits today has forced many local churches and ministries to be like that unattached arm, just lying there *lifeless!*

Some local congregations today were founded [not planted] on a verse of Scripture, a spiritual gift, talent or in some cases a song and a program. Many of these misled and dissatisfied people are running from church to church due to a situation described by C. Peter Wagner that forms the shoddy foundation upon which many traditional congregations find themselves today. In his estimation,

- Only 5% in the church are visionaries – individuals who can see the *invisibles.*
- Another 15% are implementers – who carry out the vision with little assistance.
- The other 80% need a program or guide – to help them *step* by *step* through the process.

In this paradigm, program-driven people comprise the majority, sooner or later he surmises, these people will move into leadership. If the

Spirit-led visionaries are taken away from the leadership the process will simply overtime degenerate into a *program* and soon die.

This fallacy is pronounced in many local congregations across this nation, especially in more rural and traditional settings, wherein they simply continue the program with names and date changes. The same thing applies for the order of service in many churches.

The right idea is to continuously produce faithful Spirit-led visionary leaders and implementers from within. Other problems arise between so-called local churches and Para churches such as deep mistrust and tensions due to mutual misunderstanding especially concerning true spiritual body life.

In his book *Prayer Evangelism*, Ed Silvoso stresses that neither "local church" nor "Para church" are biblical terms. And much tension arises with Para ministries because they are outside the church; however as Silvoso points out that both are valid expressions of *the* church.[23]

Blind-sided by Satan

The Bible makes it clear why all of the people in our own circles of influence have not come to Christ:

"The god of this age has blinded, those who do not believe, lest the light of the gospel of the glory of Christ, who is the image of God, should shine on them" (II Corinthians 4:4).

Satan blinds the eyes of people to the *truth* through the world system he has created. Without a godly influence, man left to himself will follow that system, which awakens the depravity of unbelievers and deepens their moral darkness (see Matthew 13:19).

It behooves the local churches and the Para ministries alike to remember God's mandate is to His universal church, the body of Christ. The Church then is the means to an end, and as such they are the means used by God to reach His end [the salvation of souls].

We praise thee O God, for the Son of thy love,
For Jesus who died and is now gone above.
All glory and praise to the Lamb that was slain,
Who has borne all our sins
And has cleansed every stain.

The writer of this great and timeless hymn, William P. Mackay, invites us to join him in "Praise" to our God for His everlasting love toward us, and may each soul be rekindled with fire from above. Our prayer is that the Lord would "revive" us again, filling each heart with His love.

And in our grateful praise for all He has done for us; the church is to spread the gospel in every area of their influence corporately and individually. Certainly we should begin in our homes, communities and to the marketplaces and beyond. There is plenty room for *every member* to be faithful, obedient and fruitful:

"Speaking the truth in love,
we are to grow up in all aspects in Him,
who is the Head, even Christ,
from whom the whole body,
being fitted and held together
by that which every joint supplies,
according to the proper working
of each individual part,
causes the growth of the body
for the building up of itself in love."
– Ephesians 4:15, 16

THERE IS A CAUSE!

We will not have to read far into the New Testament to find out that the Church today can not compare with the early Church at fulfilling the Great Commission. Why is that? Did the early Church know something that has not been revealed to the Church of the 21st century? In John 14:12, Jesus tells us,

"Most assuredly, I say to you, he who believes in Me, the works that I do He will do also; and greater works than these he will do also, because I go to My Father."

This is a key verse since it answers the "why" in the question asked in the paragraph above. Why was the Early Church able to do a much better job in fulfilling the Great Commission than the Church today?

In Acts 5:28, we see that in just a few weeks after Pentecost they were able to reach the entire city of Jerusalem with the teachings of Jesus. This certainly could not have been an easy task in the city where Jesus was crucified as a criminal and His resurrection is still discredited to this day.

Nevertheless, all of Jerusalem had been reached, and shortly thereafter the gospel had spread to all Judea, Samaria and beyond. We are told in Acts 19:10, that "this continued for two years, so that *all* who dwelt in Asia heard the word of the Lord Jesus, both Jews and Greeks." Furthermore Paul took the gospel across the Adriatic Sea from Italy, and on the Spain, because he was determined *not* to evangelize where Christ had already been preached (see Romans 15:19-23).

This tremendous expansion of the faith happened in a relatively short period of time when fierce persecution ruled the day. In spite of all history tells us that by the beginning of the fourth century, Christians had conquered the mighty Roman Empire. The Early Church had a handle on to something that we have yet to learn. Just as Jesus had promised, *"They could do greater works than He did."*

Greater works

In John 14:12-15, Jesus states that *everyone* who believes in Him should do the same works that He did. Now that He has been glorified; His disciples become bold witnesses to all the world through the power of the indwelling Holy Spirit (Acts 1:8) these works have been upgraded to *greater works.* Although debated in many theological quarters, it is a *promise* based upon one condition: **belief in Jesus.** If we believe in Jesus, we are not only entitled to do greater works than He did – we are commanded to do so! In the hour of the disciples greatest loss [Jesus' departure], He comforted them with the means that would give them the necessary resources to accomplish their task without His immediate presence. What are the greater works Jesus commands us to do?

Listen to His words, *"And whatever you ask in My name, that I will do, that the Father may be glorified in the Son"* (v. 13). To "ask in His name" certainly does not mean to tack it onto the end of a prayer as some kind of formula. It means:

1. The believer's prayer should be for Christ's kingdom purposes and not selfish reasons.
2. The believer's prayer should be on the basis of Christ's merits and not any personal merits or worthiness.

3. The believer's prayer should be in pursuit of Christ's glory alone.

PERSONAL

Have I found my place on the ministry team in our church? God has gifted me with ability for a special ministry that only I can do. God expects me to grow in character and ministry skills so I can serve Him. Things to consider:

- Your passion for ministry and various experiences God has allowed in your life.
- Look for ministry patterns that reflect God's will for your life.
- Reflect on how God has used you in the past to determine how He may use you in the future.
- Talk with your pastor or a spiritually mature Christian in your church who will help you through this process.
- Then find a place where you can begin serving God (see Matt. 9:37-38).

When you do that, the whole Church (Body) becomes stronger! Praise God!

CHAPTER 19 REVIEW: THE MINISTRY OF RECONCILIATION

1. Discuss the fact that all truly born again believers are in Christ. Apart from being "in Christ" there us absolutely no hope for any human being.
2. Discuss the peace for the believer that only comes through reconciliation. Paul wants them to remember how wonderful reconciliation really is. God has done a marvelous thing for them.
3. It is imperative that all of humanity know that the secret to peace and reconciliation with God is the cross of Christ.
4. God also gave us a word of reconciliation in all the section above we see that Paul gave us a true and trustworthy word which opposes the false and unsure one that fills the world today. Truth counters that false message.
5. In His great love and mercy God has done all He can do to help humanity escape the damnation of an eternal hell.

NOTES

INTRODUCTION

1   Romans 12:1-5
2   Jay R. Leach, *According to Pattern*, (Trafford Publishing 2016) 121
3   W. E. Vine's New Testament Greek Grammar Dictionary, (Thomas Nelson Publishers 2012) 617

NOTE: The GK word *"suschematzio"* means "to fashion or shape one thing like another" translated "conformed" in Romans 12:2 KJV and "fashioned" in I Peter 1:14.

4   Webster's New Explorer Dictionary and Thesaurs (Merriam-Webster Inc. 1999) 548

NOTE: The word means one that transforms by changing the structure, appearance or character.

5   Ray C. Stedman, *Body Life* (Glendale, Calif. Regal Books, 1972), 37

Chapter 1: The Church on Purpose

6   Letter to Diognetus, 5:1-10. *Early Christian Fathers*, translated and edited by Cyril C. Richardson, *The Library of Christian Classics*. Volume I. Philadelphia: The Westminster Press, 1953.

Chapter 2: Getting a Handle on Relity

7   W.E. Vine's New Testament Greek Grammar Dictionary, (Thomas Nelson Publishers 2012) page 617. NOTE: The Greek word *"latreuo"* means "to serve, to render homage," is translated "to worship" in Phil. 3:3; in Acts 17:25 *"therapeuo"* "to serve, do service to" (RV), is rendered "is worshipped."

8   Francis Schaffer, *The Mark of a Christian*, 2nd ed. (Dowers Grove, IL: Inter Varsity, 2006), 29.

Chapter 4: Equipping Ministry

9   **Frank Bartleman,** *Azusa Street, An Eyewitness Account,* **(Bridges-Logos, Gainsville, FL 1980) xxiv**

10 Accessed from: Secular Humanist Manifesto 2000, Secular Humanism.org/index.php 3/22/17

11 Ibid.

12 Ibid.

13 Ibid.

14 Barna Research Releases in Leaders and Pastors: "The Aging of America's Pastors" – March 1, 2017.

15 Ibid.

16 W.E. Vine's N.T. Greek Grammar Dictionary (Thoma Nelson Pub. 2012) 322

Chapter 5: Getting a Handle on Reality

17 Ed Silvoso, Anointed for Business, (Regal Books Publishers 2006) 39

Chapter 7: Is there not a Cause?

18 Secular Humanism Agenda

Chapter 8: Yes there is a Cause

19 C. S. Lewis, Mere Christianity, quoted in Martindale and Root, The Quotable Lewis, 108.

Chapter 9: Countercultural

20 Darrel Guder, *The Incarnation and the Church's Witness* (Eugene, OR: Wipf & Stock, 1999), 48-49.

Chapter 12: The Exercise of Spiritual Gifts

21 Jay R. Leach, A Light unto My Path, (Trafford Publishing 2013) 92-102

Chapter 13: God's End Strategy

22 Warren Wiersbe, Wiersbe's Expository Outlines on the New Testament (Chariot Victor Publishing 1992) 20.

23 Ed Silvoso, *Prayer Evangelism,* (Regal Books from Gospel Light 2000) 232